Advance Praise for *Predictably Irrational*

"A marvelous book that is both thought-provoking and highly entertaining, ranging from the power of placebos to the pleasures of Pepsi. Ariely unmasks the subtle but powerful tricks that our minds play on us and shows us how we can prevent being fooled."

—JEROME GROOPMAN, Professor, Harvard Medical School, and *New York Times* bestselling author of *How Doctors Think*

"This is going to be the most influential, talked-about book in years. It is so full of dazzling insights—and so engaging—that once I started reading it I couldn't put it down."

—DANIEL MCFADDEN, Nobel Laureate in Economics, 2000; Morris Cox Professor of Economics, University of California at Berkeley

"Filled with clever experiments, engaging ideas, and delightful anecdotes. Dan Ariely is a wise and amusing guide to the foibles, errors, and bloopers of everyday decision making."

—DANIEL GILBERT, Professor of Psychology, Harvard University, and *New York Times* bestselling author of *Stumbling on Happiness*

"Dan Ariely is a genius at understanding human behavior. No economist does a better job of uncovering and explaining the hidden reasons for the weird ways we act, in the marketplace and out. *Predictably Irrational* will reshape the way you see the world, and yourself, for good."

—JAMES SUROWIECKI, author of *The Wisdom of Crowds*

predictably
irrational

*The Hidden Forces That Shape
Our Decisions*

Dan Ariely

HARPER

An Imprint of HarperCollins*Publishers*
www.harpercollins.com

HarperCollins books may be purchased for educational, business, or sales promotional use. For information, please write: Special Markets Department, HarperCollins Publishers, 10 East 53rd Street, New York, NY 10022.

[Permissions TO COME.]

first edition

Designed by Renato Stanisic

Library of Congress Cataloging-in-Publication Data is available upon request.

ISBN-13: 978-0-06-135323-9

08 09 10 11 12 /RRD 10 9 8 7 6 5 4 3 2 1

To my mentors, colleagues, and students—
who make research exciting.

Contents

Introduction

*How an Injury Led Me to Irrationality and
to the Research Described Here*

I have been told by many people that I have an unusual way
of looking at the world. Over the last 20 years or so of my
research career, it's enabled me to have a lot of fun figuring out
what really influences our decisions in daily life (as opposed to
what we think, often with great confidence, influences them).

Do you know why we so often promise ourselves to diet
and exercise, only to have the thought vanish when the dessert cart rolls by?

Do you know why we sometimes find ourselves excitedly
buying things we don't really need?

Do you know why we still have a headache after taking a
five-cent aspirin, but why that same headache vanishes when
the aspirin costs 50 cents?

Do you know why people who have been asked to recall
the Ten Commandments tend to be more honest (at least immediately afterward) than those who haven't? Or why honor
codes actually do reduce dishonesty in the workplace?

By the end of this book, you'll know the answers to these and many other questions that have implications for your personal life, for your business life, and for the way you look at the world. Understanding the answer to the question about aspirin, for example, has implications not only for your choice of drugs, but for one of the biggest issues facing our society: the cost and effectiveness of health insurance. Understanding the impact of the Ten Commandments in curbing dishonesty might help prevent the next Enron-like fraud. And understanding the dynamics of impulsive eating has implications for every other impulsive decision in our lives—including why it's so hard to save money for a rainy day.

My goal, by the end of this book, is to help you fundamentally rethink what makes you and the people around you tick. I hope to lead you there by presenting a wide range of scientific experiments, findings, and anecdotes that are in many cases quite amusing. Once you see how systematic certain mistakes are—how we repeat them again and again—I think you will begin to learn how to avoid some of them.

But before I tell you about my, curious, practical, entertaining (and in some cases even delicious) research on eating, shopping, love, money, procrastination, beer, honesty, and other areas of life, I feel it is important that I tell you about the origins of my somewhat unorthodox worldview—and therefore of this book. Tragically, my introduction to this arena started with an accident many years ago that was anything but funny.

ON WHAT WOULD otherwise have been a normal Friday afternoon in the life of an eighteen-year-old Israeli, everything changed irreversibly in a matter of a few seconds. An explosion of a large magnesium flare, the kind used to illuminate battlefields at night, left 70 percent of my body covered with third-degree burns.

The next three years found me wrapped in bandages in a hospital, and then emerging into public only occasionally, dressed in a tight synthetic suit and mask that made me look like a crooked version of Spider Man. Without the ability to participate in the same daily activities as my friends and family, I felt partially separated from society and started to observe the very activities that were once my daily routine as if I were an outsider. As if I had come from a different culture (or planet), I started reflecting on the goals of different behaviors, mine and those of others. For example, I started wondering why I loved one girl but not another, why my daily routine was designed to be comfortable for the physicians but not for me, why I loved going rock climbing but not studying history, why I used to care so much about what other people thought of me, and mostly what is it about life that motivates people.

During the three years in the hospital following my accident, I had extensive experience with different types of pain, and a great deal of time between treatments and operations to reflect on it. During those long years, my daily agony was played out in the "bath," a daily procedure in which I was soaked in disinfectant solution, the bandages were removed, and the dead particles of skin were scraped off. When the skin is intact, disinfectants create a low-level sting, and in general the bandages come off easily. But when there is little or no skin—as in my case because of my extensive burns— the bandages stick to the flesh, and the disinfectant hurts like nothing else I can describe.

Early on in the burn department I started talking to the

nurses who administered my daily bath, in order to understand their approach to my treatment. The nurses would routinely grab hold of a bandage and rip it off as fast as possible, creating a relatively short burst of pain; they would repeat this process for an hour or so until they removed every one of the bandages. Once this process was over I was covered with ointment and with new bandages, in order to repeat the process again the next day.

The nurses, I quickly learned, had theorized that a vigorous tug at the bandages, which caused a sharp spike of pain, was preferable (to the patient) to a slow pulling of the wrappings, which might not lead to such a severe spike of pain but would extend the pain longer, and therefore be more painful overall. The nurses had also concluded that there was no difference between two possible methods: starting at the most painful part of the body and working their way to the least painful part; or starting at the least painful part and advancing to the most excruciating areas.

As someone who had actually experienced the pain of the bandage removal process, I did not share their beliefs (which had never been scientifically tested). Moreover, their theories gave no consideration to the amount of fear that the patient felt anticipating the treatment; to the difficulties of dealing with fluctuations of pain over time; to the unpredictability of not knowing when the pain will start and ease off; or to the benefits of being comforted with the possibility that the pain would be reduced over time. But, given my helpless position, I had little influence over any of this.

As soon as I was able to leave the hospital for a prolonged period (I would still return for occasional operations and treatments for another five years), I began studying at Tel Aviv University. During my first semester, I took a class that profoundly changed my outlook on research and largely determined my future. This was a class in the physiology of the brain, taught by professor Hanan Frenk. In addition to the fascinating material Professor Frenk presented about the workings of the brain, what struck me most about this class was his attitude to questions and alternative theories. Many times, when I raised my hand in class or stopped by his office to suggest a different interpretation of some results he had presented, he replied that my theory was indeed a possibility (somewhat unlikely, but a possibility nevertheless)—and would then challenge me to propose an empirical test to distinguish it from the conventional theory.

Coming up with such tests was not easy, but the idea that science is an empirical endeavor in which all the participants, including a new student like myself, could come up with alternative theories, as long as they found empirical ways to test these theories, opened up a new world to me. On one of my visits to Professor Frenk's office, I proposed a theory explaining how a certain stage of epilepsy developed, and included an idea for how one might test it in rats.

Professor Frenk liked the idea, and for the next three months I operated on about 50 rats, implanting catheters in their spinal cords and giving them different substances to increase or reduce their epileptic seizures. One of the practical problems with this approach was that the movements of my hands were very limited, because of my injury, and as a consequence it was very difficult for me to operate on the rats. Luckily for me, my best friend, Ron Weisberg (an avid vegetarian and animal lover), agreed to come with me to the lab for several weekends and help me with the procedures—a true test of friendship if ever there was one.

In the end, it turned out that my theory was wrong, but

this did not diminish my enthusiasm. I was able to learn something about my theory, after all, and even though the theory was wrong, it was good to know this with high certainty. I always had many questions about how things work and how people behave, and my new understanding—that science provides the tools and opportunities to examine anything I found interesting—lured me into the study of how people behave.

With these new tools, I focused much of my initial efforts on understanding how we experience pain. For obvious reasons I was most concerned with such situations as the bath treatment, in which pain must be delivered to a patient over a long period of time. Was it possible to reduce the overall agony of such pain? Over the next few years I was able to carry out a set of laboratory experiments on myself, my friends, and volunteers—using physical pain induced by heat, cold water, pressure, and loud sounds, and even the psychological pain of losing money in the stock market—to probe for the answers.

By the time I had finished, I realized that the nurses at the burn department were kind and generous individuals (well, there was one exception) with a lot of experience in soaking and removing bandages, but they still didn't have the right theory about what would minimize their patients' pain. How could they be so wrong, I wondered, considering their vast experience? Since I knew these nurses personally, I knew that their behavior was not due to maliciousness, stupidity, or neglect. Rather, they were most likely the victims of inherent biases in their perceptions of their patients' pain—biases that apparently were not altered even by their vast experience.

For these reasons, I was particularly excited when I returned to the burn department one morning and presented my results, in the hope of influencing the bandage removal procedures for other patients. It turns out, I told the nurses and physicians, that people feel less pain if treatments (such as removing bandages in a bath) are carried out with lower intensity and longer duration than if the same goal is achieved through high intensity and a shorter duration. In other words, I would have suffered less if they had pulled the bandages off slowly rather than with their quick-pull method.

The nurses were genuinely surprised by my conclusions, but I was equally surprised by what Etty, my favorite nurse, had to say. She admitted that understanding had been lacking and that they should change their methods. But she also pointed out that a discussion of the pain inflicted in the bath treatment should also take into account the psychological pain that the nurses experienced when their patients screamed in agony. Pulling the bandages quickly might be more understandable, she explained, if it were indeed the nurses' way of shortening their own torment (and their faces often did reveal that they were suffering). In the end, though, we all agreed that the procedures should be changed, and indeed, some of the nurses followed my recommendations.

My recommendations never changed the bandage removal process on a greater scale (as far as I know), but the episode left a special impression on me. If the nurses, with all their experience, misunderstood what constituted reality for the patients they cared so much about, perhaps other people similarly misunderstand the consequences of their behaviors and, for that reason, make the wrong decisions. I decided to expand my scope of research, from pain to the examination of cases in which individuals make repeated mistakes—without being able to learn much from their experiences.

THIS JOURNEY INTO the many ways in which we are all irrational, then, is what this book is about. The discipline that allows me to play with this subject matter is called *behavioral economics*.

Behavioral economics is a relatively new field, one that draws on aspects of both psychology and economics. It has led me to study everything from our reluctance to save for retirement to our inability to think clearly during sexual arousal. It's not just the behavior that I have tried to understand, though, but also the decision-making processes behind such behavior—yours, mine, and everybody else's. Before I go on, let me try to explain, briefly, what behavioral economics is all about and how it is different from standard economics. Let me start out with a bit of Shakespeare:

> *What a piece of work is a man! how noble in reason!*
> *how infinite in faculty! in form and moving how*
> *express and admirable! in action how like an angel!*
> *in apprehension how like a god! The beauty of the*
> *world, the paragon of animals.—from Act II,*
> *scene 2, of* Hamlet

The predominant view of human nature, largely shared by economists, policy makers, and nonprofessionals, everyday Joes, is the one reflected in this quotation. Of course, this view is largely correct. Our minds and bodies are capable of amazing acts. We can see a ball thrown from a distance, instantly calculate its trajectory and impact, and then move our body and hands in order to catch it. We can learn new languages with ease, particularly as young children. We can master chess. We can recognize thousands of faces without confusing them. We can produce music, literature, technology, and art—and the list goes on and on.

Shakespeare is not alone in his appreciation for the human mind. In fact, we all think of ourselves along the lines of Shakespeare's depiction (although we do realize that our neighbors, spouses, and bosses do not always live up to this standard). Within the domain of science, these assumptions of our ability for perfect reasoning have found their way into economics. In economics, this very basic idea, called *rationality*, provides the foundation for economic theories, predictions, and recommendations.

From this perspective, and to the extent that we all believe in human rationality, we are all economists. I don't mean that each of us can intuitively develop complex game-theoretical models or understand the generalized axiom of revealed preference (GARP); rather, I mean that we hold the basic beliefs about human nature on which economics is built. In this book, when I mention the *rational* economic model, I refer to the basic assumption that most economists and many of us hold about human nature—the simple and compelling idea that we are capable of making the right decisions for ourselves.

Although a feeling of awe at the capability of humans is clearly justified, there is a large difference between a deep sense of admiration and the assumption that our reasoning abilities are perfect. In fact, this book is about human *irrationality*—about our distance from perfection. I believe that recognizing where we depart from the ideal is an important part of the quest to truly understand ourselves, and one that promises many practical benefits. Understanding irrationality is important for our everyday actions and decisions, and for understanding how we design our environment and the choices it presents us with.

My further observation is that we are not only irrational, but *predictably irrational*—that our irrationality happens the same way, again and again. Whether we are acting as consumers, businesspeople, or policy makers, understanding how we are predictably irrational provides a starting point for improving our decision making, changing the way we live for the better.

This leads me to the real "rub" (as Shakespeare might have called it) between conventional economics and behavioral economics. In conventional economics, the assumption that we are all rational implies that, in everyday life, we compute the value of all the options we face and then follow the best possible path of action. What if we make a mistake and do something irrational? Here, too, traditional economics has an answer: "market forces" will sweep down on us and swiftly set us back on the path of righteousness and rationality. On the basis of these assumptions, in fact, generations of economists since Adam Smith have been able to develop far-reaching conclusions about everything from taxation and health-care policies to the pricing of good and services.

But, as you will see in this book, we are really far less rational than standard economic theory assumes. Moreover, these irrational behaviors of ours are neither random nor senseless. They are systematic, and since we repeat them again and again, predictable. So, wouldn't it make sense to modify standard economics, to move it away from naive psychology (which often fails the tests of reason, introspection, and—most important—empirical scrutiny)? This is exactly what the emerging field of behavioral economics, and this book as a small part of that enterprise, is trying to accomplish.

As YOU WILL see in the pages ahead, each of the chapters in this book is based on a few experiments I carried out over the years with some terrific colleagues (at the end of the book, I have included short biographies of my amazing collaborators). Why experiments? Life is complex, with multiple forces simultaneously exerting their influences on us, and this complexity makes it difficult to figure out exactly how each of these forces shapes our behavior. For social scientists, experiments are like microscopes or stobe lights. They help us slow human behavior to a frame-by-frame narration of events, isolate individual forces, and examine those forces carefully and in more detail. They let us test directly and unambiguously what makes us tick.

If the lessons learned in an experiment were limited to the exact environment of the experiment, their value would also be limited. Instead, I would like you to think about experiments as providing insight into how we think and how we make decisions—not only in the context of a particular experiment but, by extrapolation, in many contexts of life.

In each chapter, then, I have taken a step in extrapolating the findings from the experiments to other contexts, attempting to describe some of their implications for life, business, and public policy. The implications I have drawn are, of course, just a partial list.

To get real value from this, and from social science in general, it is important that you, the reader, spend some time thinking about how the principles of human behavior identified in the experiments apply to your life. My suggestion to you is to pause at the end of each chapter and consider whether the principles revealed in the experiments might make your life better or worse, and more importantly what you could do differently, given your new understanding of human nature. This is where the real adventure lies.

And now for the journey.

predictably
irrational

CHAPTER 1

The Truth about Relativity

Why Everything Is Relative—Even
When It Shouldn't Be

O ne day while browsing the World Wide Web (obviously
for work—not just wasting time), I stumbled on the following ad, on the Web site of a magazine, *The Economist*.

Economist.com | **SUBSCRIPTIONS**

OPINION
WORLD
BUSINESS
FINANCE & ECONOMICS
SCIENCE & TECHNOLOGY
PEOPLE
BOOKS & ARTS
MARKETS & DATA
DIVERSIONS

Welcome to
The Economist Subscription Centre
Pick the type of subscription you want to buy
or renew.

❏ **Economist.com subscription** - US $59.00
One-year subscription to Economist.com.
Includes online access to all articles from
The Economist since 1997

❏ **Print subscription** - US $125.00
One-year subscription to the print edition
of *The Economist*.

❏ **Print & web subscription** - US $125.00
One-year subscription to the print edition
of *The Economist* and online access to all
articles from *The Economist* since 1997.

I read these offers one at a time. The first offer—the Internet subscription for $59—seemed reasonable. The second option—the $125 print subscription—seemed a bit expensive, but still reasonable.

But then I read the third option: a print *and* Internet subscription for $125. I read it twice before my eye ran back to the previous options. Who would want to buy the print option alone, I wondered, when both the Internet and the print subscriptions were offered for the same price? Now, the print-only option may have been a typographical error, but I suspect that the clever people at the *Economist*'s London offices (and they are clever—and quite mischievous in a British sort of way) were actually manipulating me. I am pretty certain that they wanted me to skip the Internet-only option (which they assumed would be my choice, since I was reading the advertisement on the Web) and jump to the more expensive option: Internet and print.

But how could they manipulate me? I suspect it's because the *Economist*'s marketing wizards (and I could just picture them in their school ties and blazers) knew something important about human behavior: humans rarely choose things in absolute terms. We don't have an internal value meter that tells us how much things are worth. Rather, we focus on the relative advantage of one thing over another, and estimate value accordingly. (For instance, we don't know how much a six-cylinder car costs, but we can assume it's more expensive than the four-cylinder model).

In the case of the *Economist*, you may not have known whether the Internet-only subscription at $59 was better than the print-only option at $125. But you certainly knew that the print-and-Internet option for $125 was better than the print-only option at $125. In fact, you could reasonably deduce that in the combination package, the Internet subscription is free! "It's a bloody steal—go for it, governor!" I could almost hear them shout from the riverbanks of the Thames. And I have to admit, if I had been inclined to subscribe I probably would have taken the package deal myself. (Later, when I tested the offer on a large number of participants, the vast majority preferred the Internet-and-print deal).

So what was going on here? Let me start with a fundamental observation: most people don't know what they want unless they see it in context. We don't know what kind of racing bike we want—until we see a champ in the Tour de France ratcheting the gears on a particular model. We don't know what kind of speaker system we like—until we hear a set of speakers that sounds better than the previous one. We don't even know what we want to do with our lives—until we find a relative or a friend who is doing just what we think we should be doing. Everything is relative, and that's the point. Like an airplane pilot landing in the dark, we want runway lights on either side of us, guiding us to the place where we can touch down our wheels.

In the case of the *Economist*, the decision between the Internet-only and print-only options would take a bit of thinking. Thinking is painful. So the *Economist*'s marketers offered us a no-brainer: the print-and-Internet option.

The geniuses at the *Economist* aren't the only ones who've figured this out, however. Take Sam, the television salesman. He plays the same general type of tricks on us when he decides which televisions to put together on display:

19-inch Sylvania for $210
26-inch Sony for $385
32-inch Samsung for $580

Which one would you choose? In this case, Sam knows that customers find it difficult to compute the value of different options. (Who really knows if the Sylvania at $210 is better than the Samsung at $540?) But Sam also knows that given three choices, most people will take the middle choice (as in landing your plane between the runway lights). So guess which television Sam prices as the middle option? That's right—the one he wants to sell!

Of course, Sam is not alone in his cleverness. The *New York Times* ran a story recently about Gregg Rapp, a restaurant consultant, who gets paid to work out the pricing for menus. He knows, for instance, how lamb sold this year as opposed to last year; whether lamb did better paired with squash or with risotto; and whether orders decreased when the price of the main course was hiked from $39 to $41.

One thing Rapp has learned is that high-priced entrées on the menu boost revenues for the restaurant—even if no one buys them. Why? Because even though people generally won't buy the most expensive dish on the menu, they will order the second most expensive dish. Thus, by creating an expensive dish, a restaurateur can lure customers into ordering the second most expensive choice (which can be cleverly engineered to deliver a higher margin of profit).[1]

So LET'S RUN through the *Economist*'s sleight of hand in slow motion.

As you recall, the choices were:

1. Internet-only subscription for $59.
2. Print-only subscription for $125.
3. Print-and-Internet subscription for $125.

When I gave these options to 100 students at MIT's Sloan School of Management, they opted as follows:

1. Internet-only subscription for $59—16 students
2. Print-only subscription for $125 zero students
3. Print-and-Internet subscription for $125—84 students

So far these Sloan MBAs are smart cookies. They all saw the advantage in the print-and-Internet offer over the print-only offer. But were they influenced by the mere presence of the print-only option (which I will henceforth, and for good reason, call the "decoy"). In other words, suppose that I removed the decoy so that the choices would be the ones seen in the figure below:

Would the students respond as before (16 for the Internet only and 84 for the combination)?

Certainly they would react the same way, wouldn't they? After all, the option I took out was one that no one selected, so it should make no difference. Right?

Au contraire! This time, 68 of the students chose the Internet-only option for $59, up from 16 before. And only 32 chose the combination subscription for $125, down from 84 before.*

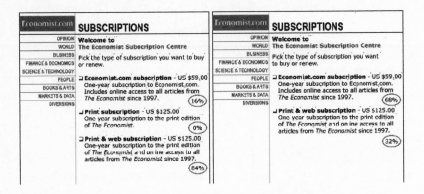

What could have possibly changed their minds? Nothing rational, I assure you. It was the mere presence of the decoy that sent 84 of them to the print-and-Internet option (and 16 to the Internet-only option). And the absence of the decoy had them choosing differently, with 32 for print-and-Internet and 68 for Internet-only.

This is not only irrational but predictably irrational as well. Why? I'm glad you asked.

---

*As a convention in this book, every time I mention that conditions are different, it is always a statistically significant difference. I refer the interested reader to the original academic papers for more details about the statistical analysis.

LET ME OFFER you this visual demonstration of relativity.

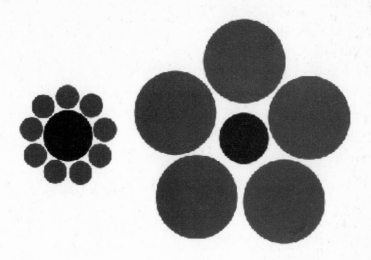

As you can see, the middle circle can't seem to stay the same size. When placed among the larger circles, it gets smaller. When placed among the smaller circles, it grows bigger. The middle circle is the same size in both positions, of course, but it appears to change depending on what we place next to it.

This might be a mere curiosity, but for the fact that it mirrors the way the mind is wired: we are always looking at the things around us in relation to others. We can't help it. This holds true not only for physical things—toasters, bicycles, puppies, restaurant entrées, and spouses—but for experiences such as vacations and educational options, and for ephemeral things as well: emotions, attitudes, and points of view.

We always compare jobs with jobs, vacations with vacations, lovers with lovers, and wines with wines. All this relativity reminds me of a line from the film *Crocodile Dundee*, when a street hoodlum pulls a switchblade against our hero, Paul Hogan. "You call that a knife?" says Hogan incredulously, withdrawing a bowie blade from the back of his boot.

"Now *this*," he says with a sly grin, "is a knife."

RELATIVITY IS (RELATIVELY) easy to understand. But there's one aspect of relativity that consistently trips us up. It's this: we not only tend to compare things with one another but also tend to focus on comparing things that are easily comparable—and to avoid comparing things that cannot be compared easily.

That may be a confusing thought, so let me give you an example. Suppose you're shopping for a house in a new town. Your real estate agent guides you to three houses, all of which interest you. One of them is a contemporary, and two are colonials. All three cost about the same; they are all equally desirable; and the only difference is that one of the colonials (the "decoy") needs a new roof and the owner has knocked a few thousand dollars off the price to cover the additional expense.

So which one will you choose?

The chances are good that you will *not* choose the contemporary and you will *not* choose the colonial that needs the new roof, but you will choose the other colonial. Why? Here's the rationale (which is actually quite irrational). We like to make decisions based on comparisons. In the case of the three houses, we don't know anything about the contemporary (we don't have another house to compare it with), so that house goes on the sidelines. But we do know that one of the colonials is better than the other one. That is, the colonial with the good roof is better than the one with the bad roof. Therefore, we will go for the colonial with the good roof, spurning the contemporary and the colonial that needs a new roof.

To better understand how relativity works, consider the following illustration:

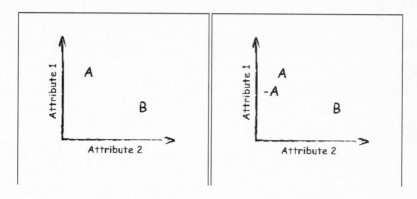

In the left side of this illustration we see two options, each of which is better on a different attribute. Option A is better on attribute 1—let's say quality. Option B is better on attribute 2—let's say price. Obviously these are two very different options and the choice between them is not simple. Now consider what happens if we add another option, called –A (see the right side of the illustration). This option is clearly worse than option A, but it is also very similar to it, making the comparison between them easy, and suggesting that A is much better than –A.

In essence, introducing –A (the decoy) creates a simple relative comparison with A, and hence makes A look better, not just relative to –A, but overall as well. As a consequence, the inclusion of –A in the set, even if no one ever selects it, makes people more likely to make A as their final choice.

Does this selection process sound familiar? Remember the pitch put together by the *Economist*? The marketers there knew that we didn't know whether we wanted an Internet subscription or a print subscription. But they figured that, of the three options, the print-and-Internet combination would be the offer we would take.

Here's another example of the decoy effect. Suppose you are planning a honeymoon in Europe. You've already decided to go to one of the major romantic cities and now have narrowed your choices to Rome and Paris, your two favorites. The travel agent presents you with the vacation packages for each city, which includes airfare, hotel accommodations, sightseeing tours, and a free gourmet breakfast every morning. Which would you select?

For most people, the decision between a week in Rome and a week in Paris is not effortless. Rome has the Coliseum; Paris, the Louvre. Both have a romantic ambience, fabulous food, and fashionable shopping. It's not an easy call. But suppose you were offered a third option: Rome without the free breakfast (called −Rome, or the decoy).

If you were to consider these three options (Paris, Rome, −Rome), you would immediately recognize that whereas Rome with the free breakfast is about as appealing to Paris with the free breakfast, the inferior option, which is Rome without the free breakfast, is a step down. The comparison between the clearly inferior option (−Rome) makes Rome with the free breakfast seem even better. In fact, −Rome makes Rome with the free breakfast look so good that you judge it to be even better than the difficult-to-compare option, Paris with the free breakfast.

ONCE YOU SEE the decoy effect in action, you realize that it is the secret agent in more decisions than we could imagine. It even helps us decide whom to date—and, ultimately, whom to marry. Let me describe an experiment that explored just this subject.

As students hurried around MIT one cold weekday, I asked some of them whether they would allow me to take their pictures for a study. In some cases, I got disapproving looks. A few students walked away. But most of them were happy to participate, and before long, the card in my digital camera was filled with images of smiling students. I returned to my office and printed 60 of them—30 of women and 30 of men.

The following week I made an unusual request of 25 of my undergraduates. I asked them to pair the 30 photographs of men and the 30 of women by physical attractiveness (matching the men with other men, and the women with other women). That is, I had them pair the Brad Pitts and the George Clooneys of MIT, as well as the Woody Allens and the Danny DeVitos (sorry, Woody and Danny). Out of these 30 pairs, I selected the six pairs—three female pairs and three male pairs—that my students seemed to agree were most alike.

Now, like Dr. Frankenstein himself, I set about giving these faces my special treatment. Using Photoshop, I mutated the pictures slightly, creating a slightly less attractive version of each of them. I found that just the slightest movement of the nose threw off the symmetry. Using another tool, I enlarged one eye, eliminated some of the hair, and added traces of acne.

No flashes of lightning illuminated my laboratory; nor was there a baying of the hounds on the moor. But this was still a good day for science. By the time I was through, I had the MIT equivalent of George Clooney in his prime (A) and the MIT equivalent of Brad Pitt in his prime (B), and also a George Clooney with a slightly drooping eye and thicker nose (–A, the decoy) and a less symmetrical version of Brad Pitt (–B, another decoy). I followed the same procedure for the less attractive pairs. I had the MIT equivalent of Woody Allen with his usual lopsided grin (A) and Woody Allen with an unnervingly misplaced eye (–A), as well as Danny DeVito (B) and a slightly disfigured version of Danny DeVito (–B).

For each of the 12 photographs, in fact, I now had a regular version as well as an inferior (−) decoy version. For an example of the two versions in the study, see the figure below (note that for this illustration, I used computerized faces, not those of the MIT students).

Version A of the study

Version B of the study

It was now time for the main part of the experiment. I took all the sets of pictures and made my way over to the student union. Approaching one student after another, I asked each to participate. When the students agreed, I handed them a sheet with three pictures (as in the illustration here). Some of them had the regular picture A, the decoy of that picture −A, and the other regular picture B. Others had the regular picture B, the decoy of that picture −B, and the other regular picture A.

For example, a set might include a regular Clooney (A), a decoy Clooney (−A), and a regular Pitt (B); or a regular Pitt (B), a decoy Pitt (−B), and a regular Clooney (A). After selecting a sheet with either male or female pictures, according to their preferences, I asked the students to circle the people they would pick to go on a date with, if they had a choice. All this took quite a while, and when I was done, I had distributed 600 sheets.

What was my motive in all this? Simply to determine if the existence of the distorted picture (−A or −B) would push my participants to choose one picture A over the other B. In other words, would a slightly less attractive George Clooney (−A) push the participants to choose the perfect George Clooney over the perfect Brad Pitt?

There were no pictures of Brad Pitt or George Clooney in my experiment, of course. The A and B pictures showed ordinary students. But do you remember how the existence of a colonial style house needing a new roof pushed people to choose a perfect colonial over a contemporary house—simply because the decoy colonial gave them something against which to compare the regular colonial? And in the *Economist*'s ad, didn't the print-only option for $125 push people to take the print-and-Internet option for $125? Similarly, would the existence of a less perfect person (–A or –B) push people to choose the perfect one (A or B), simply because the decoy option served as a point of comparison?

It did. Whenever I handed out a sheet that had a regular picture, its inferior version, and another regular picture, the participants said they would prefer to date the "regular" person—the one who was similar to but clearly superior to the distorted version—over the other, undistorted person on the sheet. This was not just a close call—it happened 75 percent of the time.

Why? To explain the decoy effect further, let me tell you something about bread-making machines. When Williams-Sonoma first introduced a home "bread bakery" machine (for $275), most consumers were not interested. What was a home bread-making machine, anyhow? Was it good or bad? Did one really need home-baked bread? Why not just buy a fancy coffeemaker sitting nearby instead? Flustered by poor sales, the manufacturer of the bread machine brought in a marketing research firm, which suggested a fix: introduce an additional model, of the bread maker one that was not only larger but priced about 50 percent higher than the initial machine.

Now sales began to rise (along with many loaves of bread), though it was not the large bread maker that was being sold. Why? Simply because consumers now had two models of bread makers to choose from. Since one was clearly larger and much more expensive than the other, people didn't have to make their decision in a vacuum. They could say: "Well, I don't know much about bread makers, but I do know that if I were to buy one, I'd rather have the smaller one for less money." And that's when bread makers began to fly off the shelves.[2]

OK for bread makers. But let's take a look at the decoy effect in a completely different situation. What about if you are single, and hope to appeal to as many attractive potential dating partners as possible at an upcoming singles event? My advice would be to bring a friend who has your basic physical characteristics (similar coloring, body type, facial features), but is slightly less attractive (−you).

Why? Because the folks you want to attract will have a hard time evaluating you with no comparables around. However, if you are compared with a −you, the decoy friend will do a lot to make you look better, not just in comparison with the decoy but also in general, and in comparison with to all the other people around. It may sound irrational (and I can't guarantee this), but the chances are good that you will get some extra attention. Of course, don't just stop at looks. If great conversation will win the day, be sure to pick a friend for the singles event who can't match your smooth delivery and rapier wit. By comparison, you'll sound great.

Now that you know this secret, be careful: when a similar but better-looking friend of the same sex asks you to accompany him or her at night, you might wonder whether you have been invited along for your company or merely as a decoy.

RELATIVITY HELPS US make decisions in life. But it also can make us downright miserable. Why? Because jealousy and envy spring from comparing our lot in life with that of others.

It was for good reason, after all, that the Ten Commandments admonished, "Neither shall you desire your neighbor's house nor field, or male of female slave, or donkey or anything that belongs to your neighbor." This might just be the toughest commandment to follow, considering that from birth we are wired to compare.

Modern life makes this weakness even more pronounced. A few years ago, for instance, I met with one of the top executives of one of the big investment companies. Over the course of our conversation he mentioned that one of his employees had recently come to him to complain about his salary.

"How long have you been with the firm?" the executive asked the young man.

"Three years. I came straight from college," was the answer.

"And when you joined us, how much did you expect to be making in three years?"

"I was hoping to be making about a hundred thousand."

The executive eyed him curiously.

"And now you are making almost three hundred thousand, so how can you possibly complain?" he asked.

"Well," the young man stammered, "it's just that a couple of the guys at the desks next to me, they're not any better than I am, and they are making three hundred ten."

The executive shook his head.

An ironic aspect of this story is that in 1993, federal securities regulators forced companies, for the first time, to reveal details about the pay and perks of their top executives. The idea was that once pay was in the open, boards would be reluctant to give executives outrageous salaries and benefits. This, it was hoped, would stop the rise in executive compensation, which neither regulation, legislation, nor shareholder pressure had been able to stop. And indeed, it needed to stop: in 1976 the average CEO was paid 36 times as much as the average worker. By 1993, the average CEO was paid 131 times as much.

But guess what happened. Once salaries became public information, the media regularly ran special stories ranking CEOs by pay. Rather than suppressing the executive perks, the publicity had CEOs in America comparing their pay with that of everyone else. In response, executives' salaries skyrocketed. The trend was further "helped" by compensation consulting firms (scathingly dubbed "Ratchet, Ratchet, and Bingo" by the investor Warren Buffett) that advised their CEO clients to demand outrageous raises. The result? Now the average CEO makes about 369 times as much as the average worker—about three times the salary before executive compensation went public.

Keeping that in mind, I had a few questions for the executive I met with.

"What would happen," I ventured, "if the information in your salary database became known throughout the company?"

The executive looked at me with alarm. "We could get over a lot of things here—insider trading, financial scandals, and the like—but if everyone knew everyone else's salary, it would be a true catastrophe. All but the highest-paid individual would feel underpaid—and I wouldn't be surprised if they went out and looked for another job."

Isn't this odd? It has been shown repeatedly that the link between amount of salary and happiness is not as strong as one would expect it to be (in fact, it is rather weak). Studies even find that countries with the "happiest" people are not among those with the highest personal income. Yet we keep pushing toward a higher salary. Much of that can be blamed on sheer envy. As H. L. Mencken, the twentieth-century journalist, satirist, social critic, cynic, and freethinker noted, a man's satisfaction with his salary depends on (Are you ready for this?) whether he makes more than his wife's sister's husband. Why the wife's sister's husband? Because (and I have a feeling that Mencken's wife kept him fully informed of her sister's husband's salary) this is a comparison that is salient and readily available.*

All this extravagance in CEOs' pay has had a damaging effect on society. Instead of causing shame, every new outrage in compensation encourages other CEOs to demand even more. "In the Web World," according to a headline in the *New York Times*, the "Rich Now Envy the Superrich."

In another news story, a physician explained that he had graduated from Harvard with the dream of someday receiving a Nobel Prize for cancer research. This was his goal. This was his dream. But a few years later, he realized that several of his colleagues were making more as medical investment advisers at Wall Street firms than he was making in medicine. He had previously been happy with his income, but hearing of his friends' yachts and vacations homes, he suddenly felt very poor. So he took another route with his career—the route of Wall Street.[3] By the time he arrived at his twentieth class reunion, making 10 times what most of his peers were making in medicine. You can almost see him, standing in the middle of the room at the reunion, drink in hand—a large circle of influence with smaller circles gathering around him. He had not won the Nobel Prize, but he had relinquished his dreams for a Wall Street salary, for a chance to stop feeling "poor." Is it any wonder that family practice

---

*Now that you know this fact, and assuming that you are not married, take this into account when you search for a soul mate. Look for someone whose sibling is married to a productivity-challenged individual.

physicians, who make an average of $160,000 a year, are in short supply?*

CAN WE DO anything about this problem of relativity?

The good news is that we can sometimes control the "circles" around us, moving toward smaller circles that boost our relative happiness. If we are at our class reunion, and there's a "big circle" in the middle of the room with a drink in his hand, boasting of his big salary, we can consciously take several steps away and talk with someone else. If we are thinking of buying a new house, we can be selective about the open houses we go to, skipping the houses that are above our means. If we are thinking about buying a new car, we can focus on the models that we can afford, and so on.

We can also change our focus from narrow to wide. Let me explain with an example from a study conducted by two brilliant researchers, Amos Tversky and Daniel Kahneman. Suppose you have two errands to run today. The first is to buy a new pen, and the second is to buy a suit for work. At an office supply store, you find a nice pen for $25. You are set to buy it, when you remember that the same pen is on sale for $18 at another store 15 minutes away. What would you do? Do you decide to take the 15-minute trip to save the $7? Most people faced with this dilemma say that they would take the trip to save the $7.

Now you are on your second task: you're shopping for your suit. You find a luxurious gray pinstripe suit for $455 and decide to buy it, but then another customer whispers in

---

*Of course, physicians have other problems as well, including insurance forms, bureaucracy, and threats of lawsuits for malpractice.

your ear that the same suit is on sale for only $448 at another store, just 15 minutes away. Do you make this second 15-minute trip? In this case, most people say that they would not.

But what is going on here? Is 15 minutes of your time worth $7, or isn't it? In reality, of course, $7 is $7—no matter how you count it. The only question you should ask yourself in these cases is whether the 15-minute trip across town, and the 15 extra minutes it would take, is worth the extra $7 you would save. Whether the amount from which this $7 will be saved is $10 or $10,000 should be irrelevant.

This is the problem of relativity—we look at our decisions in a relative way and compare them locally to the available alternative. We compare the relative advantage of the cheap pen with the expensive one, and this contrast makes it obvious to us that we should spend the extra time to save the $7. At the same time, the relative advantage of the cheaper suit is very small, so we spend the extra $7.

This is also why it is so easy for a person to add $200 to a $5,000 catering bill for a soup entrée, when the same person will clip coupons to save 25 cents on a one-dollar can of condensed soup. Similarly, why we find it easy to spend $3,000 to upgrade to leather seats on a $25,000 car, but difficult to spend the same amount on a new leather sofa (even though we know we will spend more time at home on the sofa than in the car). Yet if we just thought about this in a broader perspective, we could better assess what we could do with the $3,000 that we might spend for upgrading the car seats. Thinking broadly like this is not easy, because making relative judgments is the natural way we think. Can you get a handle on it? I know someone who can.

He is James Hong, cofounder of the Hotornot.com rating

and dating site. (James, his business partner Jim Young, Leonard Lee, George Loewenstein, and I are currently working on a research project to help determine how one's own "attractiveness" affects one's view of the "attractiveness" of others.)

For sure, James has made a lot of money, and he sees even more money all around him. One of his good friends, in fact, is a founder of PayPal and is worth tens of millions. But Hong knows how to make the circles of comparison in his life smaller, not larger. In his case, he started by selling his Porsche Boxter, buying a Toyota Prius in its place.[4]

"I don't want to live the life of a Boxter," he told the *New York Times*, "because when you get a Boxter you wish you had a 911, and you know what people who have 911s wish they had? They wish they had a Ferrari."

That's a lesson we can all learn: the more we have, the more we want. And the only cure is to break the cycle of relativity.

CHAPTER 2

The Fallacy of Supply and Demand

*Why the Price of Pearls—and Everything Else—
Is Up in the Air*

A t the onset of World War II, an Italian diamond dealer, James Assael, fled Europe for Cuba. There, he found a new livelihood: the American army needed waterproof watches, and Assael, through his contacts in Switzerland, was able to fill the demand.

When the war ended, Assael's deal with the U.S. government dried up. He was left with thousands of Swiss watches. The Japanese needed watches, of course. But they didn't have any money. They did have pearls, though—many thousands of them. Before long, Assael had taught his son how to barter Swiss watches for Japanese pearls. The business blossomed, and shortly thereafter, the son, Salvador Assael, became known as the "pearl king."

The pearl king had moored his yacht at Saint-Tropez one day in 1973, when a dashing young Frenchman, Jean-Claude

Brouillet, came aboard from an adjacent yacht. Brouillet had just sold his air-freight business and with the proceeds had purchased an atoll in French Polynesia—a blue-lagooned paradise for himself and his young Tahitian wife. Brouillet explained that its turquoise waters abounded with black-lipped oysters, *Pinctada margaritifera*. And from the black lips of those oysters came something of note: black pearls.

At the time there was no market for Tahitian black pearls, and little demand. But Brouillet persuaded Assael to go into business with him. Together they would harvest black pearls and sell them to the world. At first, Assael's marketing efforts failed. The pearls were gunmetal gray, about the size of musket balls, and he returned to Polynesia without having made a single sale. Assael could have dropped the black pearls altogether or sold them at a low price to a discount store. He could have tried to push them to consumers by bundling them together with a few white pearls. But instead Assael waited a year, until the operation had produced some better specimens, and then brought them to an old friend, Harry Winston, a legendary gemstone dealer. Winston agreed to put them in the window of his store on Fifth Avenue, with an outrageously high price tag attached. Assael, meanwhile, commissioned a full-page advertisement that ran in the glossiest of magazines. There, a string of Tahitian black pearls glowed, set among a spray of diamonds, rubies, and emeralds.

The pearls, which had shortly before been the private business of a cluster of black-lipped oysters, hanging on a rope in the Polynesian sea, were now parading through Manhattan on the arched necks of the city's most prosperous divas. Assael had taken something of dubious worth and made it fabulously fine. Or, as Mark Twain once noted about Tom

Sawyer, "Tom had discovered a great law of human action, namely, that in order to make a man covet a thing, it is only necessary to make the thing difficult to attain."

HOW DID THE pearl king do it? How did he persuade the cream of society to become passionate about Tahitian black pearls—and pay him royally for them? In order to answer this question, I need to explain something about baby geese.

A few decades ago, the naturalist Konrad Lorenz discovered that goslings, upon breaking out of their eggs, become attached to the first moving object they encounter (which is generally their mother). Lorenz knew this because in one experiment *he* became the first thing they saw, and they followed him loyally from then on. With that, Lorenz demonstrated that goslings not only make initial decisions based on what's available in their environment, but they stick with a decision once it has been made. Lorenz called this natural phenomenon *imprinting*.

Is the human brain, then, wired like that of the goose? Do our first impressions and decisions become imprinted? And if so, how does this imprinting play out in our lives? When we encounter a new product, for instance, do we accept the first price that comes before our eyes? And more importantly, does that price (which in behavioral economics we call an *anchor*) have a long-term effect on our willingness to pay for the product from then on?

It seems that what's good for the goose is good for humans as well. And this includes anchoring. From the beginning, for instance, Assael "anchored" his pearls to the finest gems in the world—and the prices followed forever after. Similarly, once we buy a new product at a particular price, we become anchored to that price. But how exactly does this work? Why do we accept anchors?

Consider this: If I asked you for the last two digits of your social security number (mine are 79), then asked you whether you would pay this number in dollars (for me this would be $79) for a particular bottle of Côtes du Rhône 1998, would the mere suggestion of that number influence how much you would be willing to spend on wine? Sounds preposterous, doesn't it? Well, wait until you see what happened to a group of MBA students at MIT a few years ago.

"Now here we have a nice Côtes du Rhône Jaboulet Parallel," said Drazen Prelec a professor at MIT's Sloan School of Management, as he lifted a bottle admiringly. "It's a 1998."

At the time, sitting before him were the 55 students from his marketing class. On this day, Drazen, George Loewenstein (a professor at Carnegie Mellon University), and I would have an unusual request for this group of future marketing pros. We would ask them to jot down the last two digits of their social security numbers. Then, we would ask them to bid on a number of items, including the bottle of wine.

What were we trying to prove? The existence of what we called *arbitrary coherence*. The basic idea of arbitrary coherence is this: although initial prices (such as the price of Assael's pearls) are "arbitrary", once those prices are established in our minds they will shape not only present prices but also future prices (this makes them "coherent"). So, would thinking about one's social security number be enough to create an anchor? That's what we wanted to see.

"For those of you who don't know much about wines," Drazen continued, "this bottle received eighty-six points from *Wine Spectator*. It has the flavor of red berry, mocha, and black chocolate; it's a medium-bodied, medium-intensity, nicely balanced red, and it makes for delightful drinking."

Drazen held up another bottle. This was a Hermitage Jaboulet La Chapelle, 1996, with a 92-point rating from the magazine *Wine Advocate*. "The finest La Chapelle since 1990," Drazen intoned, while the students looked up curiously. "Only 8,100 cases made . . ."

In turn, Drazen held up four other items: a cordless trackball (TrackMan Marble FX by Logitech); a cordless keyboard and mouse (iTouch by Logitech); a design book (*The Perfect Package: How to Add Value through Graphic Design*); and a one-pound box of Belgian chocolates by Neuhaus.

Drazen passed out forms that listed all the items. "Now I want you to write the last two digits of your social security number at the top of the page," he instructed. "And then write them again next to each of the items in the form of a price. In other words, if the last two digits are twenty-three, write twenty-three dollars."

"Now when you're finished with that," he added, "I want you to indicate on your sheets—with a simple yes or no—whether you would pay that amount for each of the products."

When the students had finished answering yes or no to each item, Drazen asked them to write down the maximum they were willing to pay for each of the products (their bids). Once they had written down their bids, the students passed the sheets up to me and I entered them into my laptop and announced the winners. One by one the student who had made the highest bid for each of the products would step up to the front of the class, pay for the product,* and take it with them.

The students enjoyed this class exercise, but when I asked them if they felt that writing down the last two digits of their social security numbers had influenced their final bids, they quickly dismissed my suggestion. No way!

When I got back to my office, I analyzed the data. Did the digits from the social security numbers serve as anchors? Remarkably, they did: the students with the highest-ending social security digits (from 80 to 99) bid highest, while those with the lowest-ending numbers (1 to 20) bid lowest. The top 20 percent, for instance, bid an average of $56 for the cordless keyboard; the bottom 20 percent bid an average of $16. In the end, we could see that students with social security numbers ending in the upper 20 percent placed bids that were 216 to 346 percent higher than those of the students with social security numbers ending in the lower 20 percent (see table below).

Now if the last two digits of your social security number are a high number I know what you must be thinking: "I've been paying too much for everything my entire life!" This is not the case, however. Social security numbers were the anchor in this experiment only because we requested them. We could have just as well asked for the current temperature or the manufacturer's suggested retail price (MSRP). Any question, in fact, would have created the anchor. Does that seem rational? Of course not. But that's the way we are—goslings,

---

*The price the highest bidder paid for an item was based not on his own bid, but on that of the second highest bidder. This is called a second price auction. William Vickrey received the Nobel prize in economics for demonstrating that this type of auction creates the conditions where it is in people's best interest to bid the maximum amount they are willing to pay for each item (this is also the general logic behind the auction system at eBay).

Average prices paid for the various products for each of the five groups of final digits in social security numbers, and the correlations between these digits and the bids submitted in the auction.

Range of last two digits of SS number	Products					
	Cordless trackball	Cordless keyboard	Design book	Neuhaus chocolates	1998 Côtes du Rhône	1996 Hermitage
00–19	$8.64	$16.09	$12.82	$9.55	$8.64	$11.73
20–39	$11.82	$26.82	$16.18	$10.64	$14.45	$22.45
40–59	$13.45	$29.27	$15.82	$12.45	$12.55	$18.09
60–79	$21.18	$34.55	$19.27	$13.27	$15.45	$24.55
80–99	$26.18	$55.64	$30.00	$20.64	$27.91	$37.55
Correlations*	0.42	0.52	0.32	0.42	0.33	0.33

*Correlation is a statistical measure of how much the movement of two variables is related. The range of possible correlations is between –1 and +1, where a correlation of 0 means that the change in value of one variable has no bearing on the change in value of the other variable.

after all.*

The data had one more interesting aspect. Although the willingness to pay for these items was arbitrary, there was also a logical, coherent aspect to it. When we looked at the bids for the two pairs of related items (the two wines and the two computer components), their relative prices seemed incredibly logical. Everyone was willing to pay more for the keyboard than for the trackball—and also pay more for the 1996 Hermitage than for the 1998 Côtes du Rhône. The significance of this is that once the participants were willing to pay a certain price for one product, their willingness to

*When I've tried this kind of experiment on executives and managers (at the MIT Executive Education Program) I've had similar success making their social security numbers influence the prices they were willing to pay for chocolates, books, and other products.

pay for other items in the same product category was judged relative to that first price (the anchor).

This, then, is what we call arbitrary coherence. Initial prices are largely "arbitrary" and can be influenced by responses to random questions; but once those prices are established in our minds, they shape not only what we are willing to pay for an item, but also how much we are willing to pay for related products (this makes them coherent).

Now I need to add one important clarification to the story I've just told. In life we are bombarded by prices. We see the manufacturer's suggested retail price (MSRP) for cars, lawn mowers, and coffeemakers. We get the real estate agent's spiel on local housing prices. But price tags by themselves are not anchors. They become anchors when we contemplate buying a product or service at that particular price. That's when the imprint is set. From then on, we are willing to accept a range of prices—but as with the pull of a bungee cord, we always refer back to the original anchor. Thus the first anchor influences not only the immediate buying decision but many others that follow.

We might see a 27-inch LCD high-definition television on sale for $600, for instance. The price tag is not the anchor. But if we decide to buy it (or seriously contemplate buying it) at that price, then the decision becomes our anchor henceforth in terms of LCD television sets. That's our peg in the ground, and from then on—whether we shop for another set or merely have a conversation at a backyard cookout—all other high-definition televisions are judged relative to that price.

Anchoring affects all kinds of purchases. Uri Simonshon (an economist at the University of Pennsylvania) and George Loewenstein, for example, found that people who move to a new city generally remain anchored to the prices they paid for housing in their former city. In their study they found for instance, that people who move from inexpensive markets (say, Lubbock, Texas) to moderately priced cities (say, Pittsburgh) don't enlarge their spending to fit the new market. Rather, these people spend an amount similar to what they were used to in the previous market, even if this means having to squeeze themselves and their families into smaller or less comfortable homes. Likewise, transplants from more expensive cities sink the same dollars into their new housing situation as they did in the past. People who move from Los Angeles to Pittsburgh, in other words, don't generally downsize their spending much once they hit Pennsylvania: they spend an amount similar to what they used to spend in Los Angeles.

It seems that we get used to the particularities of our housing markets and don't readily change. The only way out of this box, in fact, is to rent a home in the new location for a year or so. That way, we adjust to the new environment—and, after a while we are able to make a purchase that aligns with the local market.

So WE ANCHOR ourselves to initial prices. But do we hop from one anchor price to another (flip-flopping, if you will), continually changing our willingness to pay? Or does the first anchor we encounter become our anchor for a long time and for many decisions? To answer that question, we decided to conduct another experiment—one in which we attempted to lure our participants from old anchors to new ones.

For this experiment we enlisted some undergraduate students, some graduate students and some investment bankers who had come to the campus to recruit new employees for their firms. (I am not sure if the bankers understood exactly what they were about to experience, but maybe even our annoying sounds were less annoying than taking about investment banking.) Once the experiment started we presented our participants with three different sounds, and following each, asked them if they would be willing to get paid for hearing those sounds (which served as the price anchors) again. The first sound was a 30-second high-pitched 3,000-hertz sound, somewhat like someone screaming in a high-pitched voice. The second was a 30-second full-spectrum noise (also called white noise), which is similar to the noise a television set makes when there is no reception. The third was a 30-second oscillation between high-pitched and low-pitched sounds.

We used sounds because there is no existing market for annoying sounds (so the participants couldn't use a market price as a way to think about the value of these sounds). We used annoying sounds, furthermore, because no one likes such sounds (if we had used classical music, some would have liked it better than others). I selected these sounds myself, after creating hundreds of sounds, choosing these three because they were, in my opinion, equally annoying.

We placed our participants in front of computer screens at the lab, and had them clamp headphones over their ears.

As the room quieted down, the first group saw this message appear in front of them: "In a few moments we are going to play a new unpleasant tone over your headset. We are interested in how annoying you find it. Immediately after you hear the tone, we will ask you whether, hypothetically, you would be willing to repeat the same experience in exchange for a payment of 10 cents." The second group got the same message, only with an offer of 90 cents a rather than 10 cents.

Would the anchor prices make a difference? To find out, we turned on the sound—in this case the irritating 30-second, 3,000-hertz squeal. Some of our participants grimaced. Others rolled their eyes.

When the screeching ended, each participant was presented with the anchoring question, phrased as a hypothetical choice: Would the participant be willing, hypothetically, to repeat the experience for a cash payment (which was 10 cents for the first group and 90 cents for the second group)? After answering this anchoring question, the participants were asked to indicate on the computer screen the lowest price they would demand to listen to the sound again. (This decision was real, by the way, as it would determine whether they would hear the sound—and get paid for doing so.*

Soon after the participants entered their prices, they learned the outcome. Participants whose price was sufficiently low "won" the sound, had the (unpleasant) opportunity to hear it again, and got paid for doing so. The participants whose price was too high did not listen to the sound and were not paid for this part of the experiment.

What was the point of all this? We wanted to find out whether the first prices that we suggested (10 cents and 90 cents) had served as an anchor. And indeed they had. Those who first faced the hypothetical decision about whether to listen to the sound for 10 cents needed much less money to be willing to listen to this sound again (33 cents on average) relative to those who first faced the hypothetical decision about whether to listen to the sound for 90 cents—this sec-

---

*To ensure that the bids we got were indeed the lowest prices for which the participants would listen to the annoying sounds, we used the "Becker-DeGroot-Marschak procedure." This is an auction-like procedure, in which each of the participants bids against a price randomly drawn by a computer.

ond group demanded more than twice the compensation (73 cents on average) for the same annoying experience. Do you see the difference that the suggested price had?

BUT THIS WAS only the start of our exploration. We also wanted to know how strong the anchor would be in future decisions. Suppose we gave the participants an opportunity to drop this anchor and run for another? Would they do it? To put it in terms of goslings, would they swim across the pond after their original imprint and then, midway, swing their allegiance to a new mother goose? In terms of goslings, I think you know that they would stick with the original mom. But what about humans? The next two phases of the experiment would enable us to answer these questions.

In the second phase of the experiment, we took participants from the the previous 10-cent and 90-cent groups and treated them to 30 seconds of a white, wooshing noise. "Hypothetically, would you listen to this sound again for 50 cents?" we asked them at the end. The respondents pressed a button on their computers to indicate yes or no.

"OK, *how much* would you need to be paid for this?" we asked. Our participants typed in their lowest price; the computer did its thing; and, depending on their bids, some participants listened to the sound again and got paid and some did not. When we compared the prices, the 10-cents group offered much lower bids than the 90-cents group. This means that although both groups had been equally exposed to the suggested 50 cents, as their focal anchoring response (to "Hypothetically, would you listen to this sound again for 50 cents?"), the first anchor in this annoying sound category (which was 10 cents for some and 90 cents for others) predominated.

Why? I think it's because the participants in the 10-cents group said something like the following to themselves: "Well, I listened previously to that annoying sound for a low amount. This sound is not much different. So if I said a low amount for the previous one, I guess I could bear this sound for about the same price." Those who were in the 90-cents group used the same type of logic, but because their starting point was different, so was their ending point. These individuals told themselves, "Well, I listened previously to that annoying sound for a high amount. This sound is not much different. So since I said a high amount for the previous one, I guess I could bear this sound for about the same price." Indeed, the effect of the first anchor held—indicating that anchors have an enduring effect for present prices as well as for future prices.

There was one more step to this experiment. This time we had our participants listen to the oscillating sound that rose and fell in pitch for 30 seconds. We asked our 10-cents group, "Hypothetically, would you listen to this sound again for 90 cents?" And then we asked our 90-cents group, "Would you listen to this sound again for 10 cents?" Having flipped our anchors, we would now see which one exerted the greatest influence.

Once again, the participants typed in yes or no. Then we asked them for real bids: "How much would it take for you to listen to this again?" Now they had a history with three anchors: the first one they encountered in the experiment (either 10 cents or 90 cents), the second one (50 cents), and the most recent one (either 90 cents or 10 cents). Which one of these would have the largest influence on the price they demanded to listen to the sound?

Again, it was as if our participants' minds told them, "If I listened to the first sound for x cents, and listened to the second sound for x cents as well, then I can surely do this one for x cents, too!" And that's what they did. Those who had first encountered the 10-cent anchor accepted low prices, even after 90 cents was suggested as the anchor. On the other hand, those who had first encountered the 90-cent anchor kept on demanding much higher prices, regardless of the anchors that followed.

What did we show? That our first decisions resonate over a long sequence of decisions. First impressions are important, whether they involve remembering that our first DVD player cost much more than such players cost today (and realizing that, in comparison, the current prices are a steal), or remembering that gas was once a dollar a gallon, which makes every trip to the gas station a painful experience. In all these cases the random anchors that we encountered along the way and were swayed by remain with us long after the initial decision itself.

NOW THAT WE know we behave like goslings, it is important to understand the process by which our first decisions translate into long-term habits. To illustrate this process, consider this example. You're walking past a restaurant, and you see two people standing in line, waiting to get in. "This must be a good restaurant," you think to yourself. "People are standing in line." So you stand behind these people. Another person walks by. He sees three people standing in line and thinks, "This must be a fantastic restaurant," and joins the line. Others join. We call this type of behavior herding. It happens when we assume that something is good (or bad) on the basis of other people's previous behavior, and our own actions follow suit.

But there's also another kind of herding, one that we call self-herding. This happens when we believe something is good (or bad) on the basis of our own previous behavior. Essentially, once we become the first person in line at the restaurant, we begin to line up behind ourself in subsequent experiences. Does that make sense? Let me explain.

Recall your first introduction to Starbucks, perhaps several years ago. (I assume that nearly everyone has had this experience, since Starbucks sits on every corner in America.) You are sleepy and in desperate need of a liquid energy boost as you embark on an errand one afternoon. You glance through the windows at Starbucks and walk in. The prices of the coffee are a shock—you've been blissfully drinking the brew at Dunkin' Donuts for years. But since you have walked in and are now curious about what coffee at this price might taste like, you surprise yourself: you buy a small coffee, enjoy its taste and its effect on you, and walk out.

The following week you walk by Starbucks again. Should you go in? The ideal decision-making process should take into account the quality of the coffee (Starbucks versus Dunkin' Donuts); the prices at the two places; and, of course, the cost (or value) of walking a few more blocks to get to Dunkin' Donuts. This is a complex computation—so instead, you resort to the simple approach: "I went to Starbucks before, and I enjoyed myself and the coffee, so this must be a good decision for me." So you walk in and get another small cup of coffee.

In doing so, you just became the second person in line, standing behind yourself. A few days later, you again walk by Starbucks and this time, you vividly remember your past decisions and act on them again—voilà! You become the third person in line, standing behind yourself. As the weeks pass, you enter again and again and every time, you feel more strongly that you are acting on the basis of your preferences. Buying coffee at Starbucks has become a habit with you.

BUT THE STORY doesn't end there. Now that you have gotten used to paying more for coffee, and have bumped yourself up onto a new curve of consumption, other changes also become simpler. Perhaps you will now move up from the small cup for $2.20 to the medium size for $3.50 or to the Grande for $4.15. Even though you don't know how you got into this price bracket in the first place, moving to a larger coffee at a relatively greater price seems pretty logical. So is a lateral move to other offerings at Starbucks: Caffè Americano, Caffè Misto, Macchiato, and Frappuccino, for instance.

If you stopped to think about this, it would not be clear whether you should be spending all this money on coffee at Starbucks instead of getting cheaper coffee at Dunkin' Donuts or even free coffee at the office. But you don't think about these trade-offs anymore. You've already made this decision many times in the past, so you now assume that this is the way you want to spend your money. You've herded yourself—lining up behind your initial experience at Starbucks—and now you're part, of the crowd.

HOWEVER, THERE IS something odd in this story. If anchoring is based on our initial decisions, how did Starbucks manage to become an initial decision in the first place? In other words, if we were previously anchored to Dunkin' Donuts, how did we move our anchor to Starbucks? This is where it gets really interesting.

When Howard Shultz started Starbucks, he was as intuitive a businessman as Salvador Assael. He worked diligently to separate Starbucks from other coffee shops, not through price but through ambience. Accordingly, he designed Starbucks from the very beginning to feel like a continental coffeehouse.

The early shops were fragrant with the smell of roasted beans (and better-quality beans than those at Dunkin' Donuts). They sold fancy French coffee presses. The showcases presented alluring snacks—almond croissants, biscotti, raspberry custard pastries, and others. Whereas Dunkin' Donuts had small, medium and large coffees, Starbucks offered Short, Tall, Grande, and Venti, as well as drinks with high-pedigree names like Caffè Americano, Caffè Misto, Macchiato, and Frappuccino. Starbucks did everything in its power, in other words, to make the experience feel different—so different that we would not use the prices at Dunkin' Donuts as an anchor, but instead would be open to the new anchor that Starbucks was preparing for us. And that's to a great extent how Starbucks succeeded.

GEORGE, DRAZEN, AND I were so excited with the experiments on coherent arbitrariness that we decided to push the idea one step farther. This time, we had a different twist to explore.

Do you remember the famous episode in *The Adventures of Tom Sawyer*, the one in which Tom turns the whitewashing of Aunt Polly's fence into an exercise in manipulating his friends? As I'm sure you recall, Tom applies the paint with gusto, pretending to enjoy the job. "Do you call this work?" Tom tells his friends. "Does a boy get a chance to whitewash a fence every day?" Armed with this new "information," his friends discover the joys of whitewashing a fence. Before long, Tom's friends are not only paying for the privilege, but deriving real pleasure from the task—a win-win outcome if there ever was one.

From our perspective, Tom transformed a negative experience to a positive one—he transformed a situation in which compensation was required to one in which people (Tom's friends) would pay to get in on the fun. Could we do the same? We thought we'd give it a try.

One day, to the surprise of my students, I opened the day's lecture on managerial psychology with a poetry selection, a few lines of "Whoever you are holding me now in hand" from Walt Whitman's *Leaves of Grass*:

> *Whoever you are holding me now in hand,*
> *Without one thing all will be useless,*
> *I give you fair warning before you attempt me*
> *   further,*
> *I am not what you supposed, but far different.*
> *Who is he that would become my follower?*
> *Who would sign himself a candidate for my*
> *   affections?*
> *The way is suspicious, the result uncertain, perhaps*
> *   destructive,*
> *You would have to give up all else, I alone would*
> *   expect to be your*
> *   sole and exclusive standard,*
> *Your novitiate would even then be long and*
> *   exhausting,*
> *The whole past theory of your life and all*
> *   conformity to the lives*

around you would have to be abandon'd,
Therefore release me now before troubling yourself
any further, let
go your hand from my shoulders,
Put me down and depart on your way.

After closing the book, I told the students that I would be conducting three readings from Walt Whitman's *Leaves of Grass* that Friday evening: one short, one medium, and one long. Owing to limited space, I told them, I had decided to hold an auction to determine who could attend. I passed out sheets of paper so that they could bid; but before they did so, I had a question to ask them.

I asked half the students to write down whether, hypothetically, they would be willing to pay me $10 for a 10-minute recitation. I asked the other half to write down whether, hypothetically, they would be willing to listen to me recite poetry for ten minutes if I paid them $10.

This, of course, was the anchor. Now I asked the students to bid for a spot at my poetry reading. Do you think the initial anchor influenced the ensuing bids?

Before I tell you, consider two things. First, my skills at reading poetry are not of the first order. So asking someone to pay me for 10 minutes of it could be considered a stretch. Second, even though I asked the students if they would pay me for the privilege of attending the recitation, they didn't have to bid that way. They could have turned the tables completely and demanded that I pay them.

And now to the results (drumroll, please). Those who answered the hypothetical question about paying me were indeed willing to pay me for the privilege. They offered, on average, to pay me about a dollar for the short poetry reading, about two dollars for the medium poetry reading, and a bit more than three dollars for the long poetry reading. (Maybe I could make a living outside academe after all.)

But, what about those who were anchored to the thought of being paid (rather than paying me)? As you might expect, they did demand payment: on average, they wanted $1.30 to listen to the short poetry reading, $2.70 to listen to the medium poetry reading, and $4.80 to endure the long poetry reading.

Much like Tom Sawyer, then, I was able to take an ambiguous experience (and if you could hear me recite poetry, you would understand just how ambiguous this experience is) and arbitrarily make it into a pleasurable or painful experience. Neither group of students knew whether my poetry reading was of the quality that is worth paying for or of the quality that is worth listening to only if one is being financially compensated for the experience (they did not know if it is pleasurable or painful). But once the first impression had been formed (that they would pay me or that I would pay them), the die was cast and the anchor set. Moreover, once the first decision had been made, other decisions followed in what seemed to be a logical and coherent manner. The students did not know whether listening to me recite poetry was a good or bad experience, but whatever their first decision was, they used it as input for their next decisions and provided a coherent pattern of responses across the three poetry readings.

Of course, Mark Twain came to the same conclusions: "If Tom had been a great and wise philosopher, like the writer of this book, he would now have comprehended that work consists of whatever a body is obliged to do, and that play consists of whatever a body is not obliged to do." Mark Twain further observed: "There are wealthy gentleman in England who drive four-horse passenger-coaches twenty or thirty miles on a daily line in the summer because the privilege costs them considerable money; but if they were offered wages for the service, that would turn it into work, and then they would resign."*

WHERE DO THESE thoughts lead us? For one, they illustrate the many choices we make, from the trivial to the profound, in which anchoring plays a role. We decide whether or not to purchase Big Macs, smoke, run red lights, take vacations in Patagonia, listen to Tchaikovsky, slave away at doctoral dissertations, marry, have children, live in the suburbs, vote Republican, and so on. According to economic theory, we base these decisions on our fundamental values—our likes and dislikes.

But what are the main lessons from these experiments about our lives in general? Could it be that the lives we have so carefully crafted are largely just a product of arbitrary coherence? Could it be that we made arbitrary decisions at some point in the past (like the goslings adopting Lorenz as their parent) and have built our lives on them ever since, assuming that the original decisions were wise? Is that how we chose our careers, our spouses, the clothes we wear, and the way we style our hair? Were they smart decisions in the first place? Or were they partially random first imprints that have run wild?

Descartes said, *Cogito ergo sum*—"I think, therefore I am." But suppose we are nothing more than the sum of our first, naive, random behaviors. What then?

These questions may be tough nuts to crack, but in terms

---

*We will return to this astute observation in the chapter on social and market norms (Chapter 4).

of our personal lives, we can actively improve on our irrational behaviors. We can start by becoming aware of our vulnerabilities. Suppose you're planning to buy a cutting-edge cell phone (the one with the three-megapixel, 8× zoom digital camera), or even a daily $4 cup of gourmet coffee. You might begin by questioning that habit. How did it begin? Second, ask yourself what amount of pleasure you will be getting out of it. Is the pleasure as much as you thought you would get? Could you cut back a little and spend the remaining money better, on something else? With everything you do, in fact, you should train yourself to question your repeated behaviors. In the case of the cell phone, could you take a step back from the cutting edge, reduce your outlay, and use some of the money for something else? And as for the coffee—rather than asking which blend of coffee you will have today, ask yourself whether you should even be having that habitual cup of expensive coffee at all.

We should also pay particular attention to the first decision we make in what is going to be a long stream of decisions (about clothing, food, etc.). When we face such a decision, it might seem to us that this is just one decision, without large consequences; but in fact the power of the first decision can have such a long-lasting effect that will percolate into our future decisions for years to come. Given this effect, the first decision is crucial, and we should give it an appropriate amount of attention.

Socrates said that the unexamined life is not worth living. Perhaps it's time to inventory the imprints and anchors in our own life. Even if they once were completely reasonable, are they still reasonable? Once the old choices are reconsidered, we can open ourselves to new decisions—and the new opportunities of a new day. That seems to make sense.

ALL THIS TALK about anchors and goslings has larger implications than consumer preferences, however. Traditional
economics assumes that prices of products in the market are
determined by a balance between two forces: production at
each price (supply) and the desires of those with purchasing
power at each price (demand). The price at which these two
forces meet determines the prices in the marketplace.

This is an elegant idea, but it depends centrally on the assumption that the two forces are independent and that together they produce the market price. The results of all the
experiments presented in this chapter (and the basic idea of
arbitrary coherence itself) challenge these assumptions. First,
according to the standard economic framework, consumers'
willingness to pay is one of the two inputs that determine
market prices (this is the demand). But as our experiments
demonstrate, what consumers are willing to pay can easily be
manipulated, and this means that consumers don't in fact
have a good handle on their own preferences and the prices
they are willing to pay for different goods and experiences.

Second, whereas the standard economic framework assumes that the forces of supply and demand are independent,
the type of anchoring manipulations we have shown here
suggest that they are in fact dependent. In the real world,
anchoring comes from manufacturer's suggested retail prices
(MSRPs), advertised prices, promotions, product introduc-
tions, etc.—all of which are supply-side variables. It seems
then that instead of consumers' willingness to pay influencing market prices, the causality is somewhat reversed and it is
market prices themselves that influence consumers' willingness to pay. What this means is that demand is not, in fact, a
completely separate force from supply.

AND THIS IS not the end of the story. In the framework of arbitrary coherence, the relationships we see in the marketplace between demand and supply (for example, buying more yogurt when it is discounted) are based not on preferences but on memory! Here is an illustration of this idea. Consider your current consumption of milk and wine. Now imagine that two new taxes will be introduced tomorrow. One will cut the price of wine by 50 percent, and the other will increase the price of milk by 100 percent. What do you think will happen? These price changes will surely affect consumption, and many people will walk around slightly happier and with less calcium. But now imagine this. What if the new taxes are accompanied by induced amnesia for the previous prices of wine and milk? What if the prices change in the same way, but you do not remember what you paid for these two products in the past?

I suspect that the price changes would make a huge impact on demand if people remembered the previous prices and noticed the price increases; but I also suspect that without a memory for past prices, these price changes would have a trivial effect, if any, on demand. If people had no memory of past prices, the consumption of milk and wine would remain essentially the same, as if the prices had not changed. In other words, the sensitivity we show to price changes might in fact be largely a result of our memory for the prices we have paid in the past and our desire for coherence with our past decisions—not at all a reflection of our true preferences or our level of demand.

The same basic principle would also apply if the government, one day decided to impose a tax that doubled the price of gasoline. Under conventional economic theory, this should cut demand. But would it? Certainly, people would initially compare the new prices with their anchor, would be flabbergasted by the new prices, and so might pull back on their gasoline consumption and maybe even get a hybrid car. But over the long run, and once consumers readjusted to the new price and the new anchors (just as we adjust to the price of Nike sneakers, bottled water, and everything else) our gasoline consumption, at the new price, might in fact get close to the pretax level. Moreover, much as in the example of Starbucks, this process of readjustment could be accelerated if the price change were to also be accompanied by other changes, such as a new grade of gas, or a new type of fuel (such as corn-based ethanol fuel).

I am not suggesting that doubling the price of gasoline would have no effect on demand. But, I do believe that in the long term, it would have a much smaller influence on demand than would be assumed from just observing the short-term market reactions to price increases.

ANOTHER IMPLICATION OF arbitrary coherence has to do with the claimed benefits of the free market and free trade. The basic idea of the free market is that if I have something that you value more than I do—let's say a sofa—trading this item will benefit both of us. This means that the mutual benefit of trading rests on the assumption that all the players in the market know the value of what they have and the value of the things they are considering getting from the trade.

But if our choices are often affected by random initial anchors, as we observed in our experiments, the choices and trades we make are not necessarily going to be an accurate reflection of the real pleasure or utility we derive from those products. In other words, in many cases we make decisions in the marketplace that may not reflect how much we value different items. Now, if we can't accurately compute these pleasure values, but frequently follow arbitrary anchors instead, than it is not clear that the opportunity to trade is necessarily going to make us better off. For example, because of some unfortunate initial anchors we might mistakenly trade something that truly gives us a lot of pleasure (but regrettably had a low initial anchor) for something that gives us less pleasure (but owing to some random circumstances had a high initial anchor). If anchors and memories of these anchors—but not preferences—determine our behavior, why would trading be hailed as the key to maximizing personal happiness (utility)?

So, WHERE DOES this leave us? If we can't rely on the market forces of supply and demand to set optimal market prices, and we can't count on free-market mechanisms to help us maximize our utility, then we may need to look elsewhere. This is, especially the case with society's essentials, such as health care, medicine, water, electricity, education, and other critical resources. If you accept the premise that market forces and free markets will not always regulate the market for the best, then you may find yourself among those who believe that the government (we hope a reasonable and thoughtful government) must play a larger role in regulating some market activities, even if this limits free enterprise. Yes, a free market based on supply, demand, and no friction would be the ideal if we were truly rational. But when we are not rational but irrational, policies should take this important factor into account.

CHAPTER 3

The Cost of Zero Cost

*Why We Often Pay Too Much When
We Pay Nothing*

Have you ever grabbed for a coupon offering a free! package of coffee beans—even though you don't drink coffee and don't even have a machine with which to brew it? What about all those free! extra helpings you piled on your plate at a buffet, even though your stomach had already starting to ache from all the food you had already consumed? And what about the worthless free! stuff you've accumulated—the promotional T-shirt from the radio station, the teddy bear that came with the box of Valentine chocolates, the magnetic calendar your insurance agent sends you each year?

It's no secret that getting something free feels very good. Zero is not just another price, it turns out. Zero is an emotional hot button—a source of irrational excitement. Would you buy something if it were discounted from 50 cents to 20 cents? Maybe. Would you buy it if it were discounted from 50 cents to two cents? Maybe. Would you grab it if it were discounted from 50 cents to zero? You bet!

What is it about zero cost that we find so irresistible? Why does free! make us so happy? After all, free! can lead us into trouble: things that we would never consider purchasing become incredibly appealing as soon as they are free. For instance, have you ever gathered up free pencils, key chains, and notepads at a conference, even though you'd have to carry them home and would only throw most of them away? Have you ever stood in line for a very long time (too long), just to get a free cone of Ben and Jerry's ice cream? Or have you bought two of a product that you wouldn't have chosen in the first place, just to get the third one for free?

ZERO HAS HAD a long history. The Babylonians invented the concept of zero; the ancient Greeks debated it in lofty terms (how could something be nothing?); the ancient Indian scholar Pingala paired zero with the numeral 1 to get double digits; and both the Mayans and the Romans made zero part of their numeral systems. But zero really found its place about AD 498, when the Indian astronomer Aryabhata sat up in bed one morning and exclaimed, *"Sthanam sthanam dasa gunam"*—which translates, roughly, as "Place to place in 10 times in value." With that, the idea of decimal-based place-value notation was born. Now zero was on a roll: It spread to the Arab world, where it flourished; crossed the Iberian Peninsula to Europe (thanks to the Spanish Moors); got some tweaking from the Italians; and eventually sailed the Atlantic to the New World, where zero ultimately found plenty of employment (together with the digit 1) in a place called Silicon Valley.

So much for a brief recounting of the history of zero. But the concept of zero applied to money is less clearly understood. In fact, I don't think it even has a history. Nonetheless, free! has huge implications, extending not only to discount prices and promotions, but also to how free! can be used to help us make decisions that would benefit ourselves and society.

If free! were a virus or a subatomic particle, I might use an electron microscope to probe the object under the lens, stain it with different compounds to reveal its nature, or somehow slice it apart to reveal its inner composition. In behavioral economics we use a different instrument, however—one that allows us to slow down human behavior and examine it frame by frame, as it unfolds. As you have undoubtedly guessed by now, this procedure is called an experiment.

IN ONE EXPERIMENT, Kristina Shampanier (a PhD student at MIT) and I went into the chocolate business. Well, sort of. We set up a table at a large public building and offered two kinds of chocolates—Lindt truffles and Hershey's Kisses. There was a large sign above our table that read, "One chocolate per customer." Once the potential customers stepped closer, they could see the two types of chocolate and their prices.*

For those of you who are not chocolate connoisseurs, Lindt is produced by a Swiss firm that has been blending fine cocoas for 160 years. Lindt's chocolate truffles are particularly prized—exquisitely creamy and just about irresistible. They cost, about 50 cents each when we buy them in bulk. Hershey's Kisses, on the other hand, are good little choco-

---

*We posted the prices so that they were visible only when people got close to the table. We did this because we wanted to make sure that we did not attract different types of people in the different conditions—avoiding what is called self-selection.

lates, but let's face it, they are rather ordinary: Hershey cranks out 80 million Kisses a day. In Hershey, Pennsylvania, even the street lamps are made in the shape of the ubiquitous Hershey's Kiss.

So what happened when the students flocked to our table? When we set the price of a Lindt truffle at 15 cents and a Kiss at one cent, we were not surprised to find that our customers acted with a good deal of rationality: they compared the price and quality of the Kiss with the price and quality of the truffle, and then made their choice. About 73 percent of them chose the truffle and 27 percent chose a Kiss.

Now we decided to see how free! might change the situation. So we offered the Lindt truffle for 14 cents and the Kisses free! Would there be a difference? Should there be? After all, we had merely lowered the price of both kinds of chocolate by one cent.

But what a difference free! made. The humble Hershey's Kiss became a big favorite. Some 69 percent of our customers (up from 27 percent before) chose the FREE! Kiss. Meanwhile, the Lindt truffle took a tumble; customers choosing it decreased from 73 to 31 percent.

What was going on here? First of all, let me say that there are many times when getting free! items can make perfect sense. If you find a bin of free athletic socks at a department store, for instance, there's no downside to grabbing all the socks you can. The critical issue arises when free! becomes a struggle between a free item and another item—a struggle in which the presence of free! leads us to make a bad decision. For instance, imagine going to a sports store to buy a pair of white socks, the kind with a nicely padded heel and a gold toe. Fifteen minutes later you're leaving the store, not with the socks you came in for, but with a cheaper pair that you don't like at all (without a padded heel and gold toe) but that came in a package with a free! second pair. This is a case in which you gave up a better deal and settled for something that was not what you wanted, just because you were taken by the free!

To replicate this experience in our chocolate experiment, we told our customers that they could choose only a single sweet—the Kiss or the truffle. It was an either-or decision, like choosing one kind of athletic sock over another. That's what made the customers' reaction to the free! Kiss so dramatic: Both chocolates were discounted by the same amount of money. The relative price difference between the two was unchanged—and so was the expected pleasure from the two.

According to standard economic theory, then, the price reduction should not lead to any change in the behavior of our customers. Before, about 27 percent chose the Kiss and 73 percent chose the truffle. And since nothing had changed in relative terms, the response to the price reduction should have been exactly the same. A passing economist, twirling his cane and espousing conventional economic theory, in fact, would have said that since everything in the situation was the same, our customers should have chosen the truffles by the same margin of preference.*

And yet here we were, with people pressing up to the table to grab our Hershey's Kisses, not because they had made a reasoned cost-benefit decision before elbowing their way in, but simply because the Kisses were free! How strange (but predictable) we humans are!

---

*For a more detailed account of how a rational consumer should make decisions in these cases, see the appendix to this chapter.

THIS CONCLUSION, INCIDENTALLY, remained the same in other experiments as well. In one case we priced the Hershey's Kiss at two cents, one cent, and zero cents, while pricing the truffle correspondingly at 27 cents, 26 cents, and 25 cents. We did this to see if discounting the Kiss from two cents to one cent and the truffle from 27 cents to 26 cents would make a difference in the proportion of buyers for each. It didn't. But, once again, when we lowered the price of the Kiss to free! the reaction was dramatic. The shoppers overwhelmingly demanded the Kisses.

We decided that perhaps the experiment had been tainted, since shoppers may not feel like searching for change in a purse or backpack, or they may not have any money on them. Such an effect would artificially make the free offer seem more attractive. To address this possibility, we ran other experiments at some of the MIT cafeterias. In this setup, the chocolates were displayed next to the cashier as one of the cafeteria's regular promotions and the students who were interested in the chocolates simply added them to the lunch purchase, and paid for them while going through the cashier's line. What happened? The students still went overwhelmingly for the free! option.

WHAT IS IT about free! that's so enticing? Why do we have an irrational urge to jump for a free! item, even when it's not what we really want?

I believe the answer is this. Most transactions have an upside and a downside, but when something is free! we forget the downside. free! gives us such an emotional charge that we perceive what is being offered as immensely more valuable than it really is. Why? I think it's because humans are intrinsically afraid of loss. The real allure of free! is tied to this fear. There's no visible possibility of loss when we choose a free! item (it's free). But suppose we choose the item that's *not* free. Uh-oh, now there's a risk of having made a poor decision—the possibility of a loss. And so, given the choice, we go for what is free.

For this reason, in the land of pricing, zero is not just another price. Sure, 10 cents can make a huge difference in demand (suppose you were selling millions of barrels of oil), but nothing beats the emotional surge of free! This, the *zero price effect*, is in a category all its own.

To be sure, "buying something for nothing" is a bit of an oxymoron. But let me give you an example of how we often fall into the trap of buying something we may not want, simply because of that sticky substance, free!

I recently saw a newspaper ad from a major electronics maker, offering me seven free! DVD titles if I purchased the maker's new high-definition DVD player. First of all, do I need a high-definition player right now? Probably not, because very few DVDs are recorded in high definition. But even if I did, wouldn't it be wiser to wait for prices to descend? They always do—and today's $600 high-definition DVD player will very quickly be tomorrow's $200 machine. Second, the DVD maker had a clear agenda behind its offer. This company's high-definition DVD system is in cutthroat competition with Blu-Ray, a system backed by many other manufacturers. Right now, Blu-Ray is ahead and could possibly dominate the market. So how much is free! when the machine being offered may find its way into obsolescence (like Beta VHS)? Those are two rational thoughts, at least, that might prevent us from falling under the spell of free! But, gee, those free! DVDs certainly look good!

GETTING SOMETHING FREE! is certainly a draw when we talk about prices. But what would happen if the offer was not a free price, but a free exchange? Are we as susceptible to free products as we are to getting products for free? A few years ago, with Halloween drawing near, I had an idea for an experiment to probe that question. This time I wouldn't even have to leave my home to get my answers.

Early in the evening, Joey, a nine-year-old kid dressed in a Spiderman outfit with a mask and black point Caps, and carrying a large yellow bag, climbed the stairs of our front porch. His mother accompanied him, to ensure that no one gave her kid an apple with a razor blade inside. (By the way, there never was a case of razor blades being distributed in apples on Halloween; it is just an urban myth.) She stayed on the sidewalk, however, to give Joey the feeling that he was trick-or-treating by himself.

After the traditional query, "Trick or treat?" I asked Joey to hold open his right hand. I placed three Hershey's Kisses in his palm and asked him to hold them there for a moment. "You can also get one of these two Snickers bars," I said, showing him a small one and a large one. "In fact, if you give me one of those Hershey's Kisses I will give you this smaller Snickers bar. And if you give me two of your Hershey's Kisses, I will give you this larger Snickers bar."

Now a kid may dress up like a giant spider, but that doesn't mean he's stupid. The small Snickers bar weighed one ounce, and the large Snickers bar weighed two ounces. All Joey had to do was give me one additional Hershey's Kiss (about 0.16 ounce) and he would get an extra ounce of Snickers. This deal might have stumped a rocket scientist, but for a nine-year-old boy, the computation was easy: he'd get more than six times the return on investment (in the net weight of chocolate) if he went for the larger Snickers bar. In a flash Joey put two of his Kisses into my hand, took the two-ounce Snickers bar, and dropped it into his bag.

Joey wasn't alone in making this snap decision. All but one of the kids to whom I presented this offer traded in the Kisses for the bigger candy bars.

Zoe was the next kid to walk down the street. She was dressed as a princess, in a long white dress, with a magic wand in one hand and an orange Halloween pumpkin bucket in the other. Her younger sister was resting comfortably in their father's arms, looking cute and cuddly in her bunny outfit. As they approached, Zoe called out, in a high, cute voice, "Trick or treat!" In the past I admit that I have sometimes devilishly replied, "Trick!" Most kids stand there, baffled, having never thought through their question to see that it allowed an alternative answer.

In this case I gave Zoe her treat—three Hershey's Kisses. But I did have a trick up my sleeve. I offered little Zoe a deal: a choice between getting a large Snickers bar in exchange for one of her Hershey's Kisses, or getting the small Snickers bar for free! without giving up any Hershey's Kisses.

Now, a bit of rational calculation (which in Joey's case was amply demonstrated) would show that the best deal is to forgo the free small Snickers bar, pay the cost of one additional Hershey's Kiss, and go for the large Snickers bar. On an ounce for ounce, chocolate comparison, it was far better to give up one little Hershey's Kiss and get the larger Snickers bar (two ounces) instead of a smaller Snicker's bar (one ounce). This logic was perfectly clear to Joe and the kids who encountered the condition in which both Snickers bars had a cost. But what would Zoe do? Would her clever kid's mind take that rational choice—or would the fact that the small Snicker's bar was free! blind her to the rationally right answer?

As you might have guessed by now, Zoe, and the other kids to whom I offered the same deal, were completely blinded by free! About 70 percent of them gave up the better deal, and took the worse deal just because it was free!

Just in case you think Kristina and I make a habit of picking on kids, I'll mention that we repeated the experiment with bigger kids, in fact students at the MIT student center. The results replicated the pattern we saw on Halloween. Indeed, the draw of zero cost is not limited to monetary transactions. Whether it's products or money, we just can't resist the gravitational pull of free!

So DO YOU think you have a handle on free!?

OK. Here's a quiz. Suppose I offered you a choice between a $10 Amazon gift certificate free! and a $20 gift certificate for seven dollars. Think quickly. Which would you take?

If you jumped for the free! certificate, you would have been like most of the people we tested at one of the malls in Boston. But look again: a $20 gift certificate for seven dollars delivers a $13 profit. That's clearly better than getting a $10 certificate free (earning $10). Can you see the irrational behavior in action?*

LET ME TELL you a story that describes the real influence of free! on our behavior. A few years ago, Amazon.com started

---

*We also conducted the experiment offering the $10 gift certificate for one dollar and the $20 certificate for eight dollars. This time most of the participants jumped for the $20 certificate.

offering free! shipping of orders over a certain amount. Someone who purchased a single book for $16.95 might pay an additional $3.95 for shipping, for instance. But if the customer bought another book, for a total of $31.90, they would get their shipping free!

Some of the purchasers probably didn't want the second book (and I am talking here from personal experience) but the free! shipping was so tempting that to get it, they were willing to pay the cost of the extra book. The people at Amazon were very happy with this offer, but they noticed that in one place—France—there was no increase in sales. Is the French consumer more rational than the rest of us? Unlikely. Rather, it turned out, the French customers were reacting to a different deal.

Here's what happened. Instead of offering shipping free! on orders over a certain amount, the French division priced the shipping for those orders at one franc. Just one franc—about 20 cents. This doesn't seem very different from free! but it was. In fact, when Amazon changed the promotion in France to include free! shipping, France joined all the other countries in a dramatic sales increase. In other words, whereas shipping for one franc—a real bargain—was virtually ignored by the French, free! shipping caused an enthusiastic response.

America Online (AOL) had a similar experience several years ago when it switched from pay-per-hour service to a monthly payment schedule (in which you could log in as many hours as you wanted for a fixed $19.95 per month). In preparation for the new price structure, AOL geared up for what it estimated would be a five percent increase in demand. What did it get? An overnight increase from 140,000 to 236,000 customers logging into the system, and a doubling of the average time online. That may seem good—but it wasn't good. AOL's customers encountered busy phone lines, and soon AOL was forced to lease services from other online providers (who were only too happy to sell bandwidth to AOL—at the premium of snow shovels in a snowstorm). What Bob Pittman (the president of AOL at the time) didn't realize was that consumers would respond to the allure of free! like starving people at a buffet.

WHEN CHOOSING BETWEEN two products, then, we often overreact to the free one. We might opt for a FREE! checking account (with no benefits attached) rather than one that costs five dollars a month. But if the five-dollar checking account includes free traveler's checks, online billing, etc., and the free! one doesn't, we may end up spending more for this package of services with the free! account than with the five-dollar account. Similarly, we might choose a mortgage with no closing costs, but with interest rates and fees that are off the wall; and we might get a product we don't really want simply because it comes with a free gift.

My most recent personal encounter with this involved a car. When I was looking for a new car last year, I knew that I really should buy a minivan. In fact, I had read up on Honda minivans and knew all about them. But then an Audi caught my eye, at first through an appealing offer—free! oil changes for the next three years. How could I resist?

To be perfectly honest, the Audi was sporty and red, and I was still resisting the idea of being a mature and responsible father to two young kids. It wasn't as if the free oil change completely swayed me, but its influence on me was, from a rational perspective, unjustifiably large. Just because it was free! it served as an additional allure that I could cling to.

So I bought the Audi—and the free! oil. (A few months later, while I was driving on a highway, the transmission broke—but that is a different story.) Of course, with a cooler head I might have made a more rational calculation. I drive about 7,000 miles a year; the oil needs to be changed every 10,000 miles; and the cost per change is about $75. Over three years, then, I would save about $150, or about 0.5 percent of the purchase price of the car—not a good reason to base my decision on. It gets worse, though: now I have an Audi that is packed to the ceiling with action figures, a stroller, a bike, and other kids' paraphernalia. Oh, for a minivan.

THE CONCEPT OF zero also applies to time. Time spent on one activity, after all, is time taken away from another. So if we spend 45 minutes in a line waiting for our turn to get a free! taste of ice cream, or if we spend half an hour filling out a long form for a tiny rebate, there is something else that we are not doing with our time.

My favorite personal example is free-entrance day at a museum. Despite the fact that most museums are not very expensive, I find it much more appealing to satisfy my desire for art when the price is zero. Of course I am not alone in this desire. So on these days I usually find that the museum is overcrowded, the line is long, it is hard to see anything, and fighting the crowds around the museum and in the cafeteria is unpleasant. Do I realize that it is a mistake to go to a museum when it is free? You bet I do—but I go nevertheless.

ZERO MAY ALSO affect food purchases. Food manufacturers have to convey all kinds of information on the side of the box. They have to tell us about the calories, fat content, fiber, etc. Is it possible that the same attraction we have to zero price could also apply to zero calories, zero trans fats, zero carbs, etc.? If the same general rules apply, Pepsi will sell more cans if the label says "zero calories" than if it says "one calorie."

Suppose you are at a bar, enjoying a conversation with some friends. With one brand you get a calorie-free beer, and with another you get a three-calorie beer. Which brand will make you feel that you are drinking a really light beer? Even though the difference between the two beers is negligible, the zero-calorie beer will make you feel that you're doing the right thing, healthwise. You might even feel so good that you go ahead and order a plate of fries.

So YOU CAN maintain the status quo with a 20-cent fee (as in the case of the Amazon's shipping in France), or you can start a stampede by offering something for free! Think how powerful that idea is! Zero is not just another discount. Zero is a different place. The difference between two cents and one cent is small. But the difference between one cent and zero is huge!

If you are in business, and understand that, you can do some marvelous things. Want to draw a crowd? Make something free! Want to sell more products? Make part of the purchase free!

Similarly, we can use free! to drive social policy. Want people to drive electric cars? Don't just lower the registration and inspection fees—eliminate them, so that you have created free! In the same way, if health is your concern, focus on early detection as a way to eliminate the progression of severe illnesses. Want people to do the right thing—in terms of getting regular colonoscopies, mammograms, cholesterol checks, diabetes checks, and such? Don't just decrease the cost (by decreasing the co-pay). Make these critical procedures free!

I don't think most policy strategists realize that free! is a card in their hand, let alone know how to play it. It's certainly counterintuitive, in these times of budget cutbacks, to make something free! But when we stop to think about it, can have a great deal of power, and it makes a lot of sense.

APPENDIX: CHAPTER 3

Let me explain how the logic of standard economic theory would apply to our setting. When a person can select one and only one of two chocolates, he needs to consider not the absolute value of each chocolate but its relative value—what he gets and what he gives up. As a first step the rational consumer needs to compute the relative net benefits of the two chocolates (the value of the expected taste minus the cost), and make a decision based on which chocolate has the larger net benefit. How would this look when the cost of the Lindt truffles was 15 cents and the cost of the Kiss was one cent? The rational consumer would estimate the amount of pleasure he expects to get from the truffle and the Kiss (let's say this is 50 and five pleasure units, respectively) and subtract the displeasure he would get from paying 15 cents and one cent (let's say this is 15 displeasure units and one displeasure unit, respectively). This would give him a total expected pleasure of 35 pleasure units (50−15) for the truffle, and a total expected pleasure of four pleasure units (5−1) for the Kiss.

The truffle leads by 31 points, so it's an easy choice—the truffle wins hands down.

What about the case when the cost is reduced by the same amount for both products? (Truffles cost 14 cents and the Kiss is free.) The same logic applies. The taste of the chocolates has not changed, so the rational consumer would estimate the pleasure to be 50 and five pleasure units, respectively. What has changed is the displeasure. In this setting the rational consumer would have a lower level of displeasure for both chocolates because the prices have been reduced by one cent (and one displeasure unit). Here is the main point: because both products were discounted by the same amount, their relative difference would be unchanged. The total expected pleasure for the truffle would now be 36 pleasure units (50−14), and the total expected pleasure for the Kiss would now be five pleasure units (5−0). The truffle, still leads by 31 points, so it should be the same easy choice. The truffle wins hands down.

This is how the pattern of choice should look, if the only forces at play were those of a rational cost-benefit analysis. The fact that the results from our experiments are so different tells us loud and clear that something else is going on.

CHAPTER 4

The Cost of Social Norms

*Why We Are Happy to Do Things, but Not
When We Are Paid to Do Them*

Y ou are at your mother-in-law's house for Thanksgiving
dinner, and what a sumptuous spread she has put on the
table for you! The turkey is roasted to a golden brown; the
stuffing is homemade and exactly the way you like it. Your
kids are delighted: the sweet potatoes are crowned with
marshmallows. And your wife is flattered: her favorite recipe
for pumpkin pie has been chosen for dessert.

The festivities continue into the late afternoon. You loosen
your belt and sip a glass of wine. Gazing fondly across the
table at your mother-in-law, you rise to your feet and pull out
your wallet. "Mom, for all the love you've put into this, how
much do I owe you?" you say sincerely. As silence descends
on the gathering, you wave a handful of bills. "Do you think
three hundred dollars will do it? No, wait, I should give you
four hundred!"

This is not a picture that Norman Rockwell would have
painted. A glass of wine falls over; your mother-in-law stands

up red-faced; your sister-in-law shoots you an angry look; and your niece bursts into tears. Next year's Thanksgiving celebration, it seems, may be a frozen dinner in front of the television set.

WHAT'S GOING ON here? Why does an offer for direct payment put such a damper on the party? The answer is that we live simultaneously in two different worlds—one where social norms prevail, and the other where market norms make the rules. The social norms include the friendly requests that people make of one another. Could you help me move this couch? Could you help me change this tire? Social norms are wrapped up in our social nature and our need for community. They are usually warm and fuzzy. Instant paybacks are not required: you may move your neighbor's couch, but this doesn't mean he has to come right over and move yours. It's like opening a door for someone: it provides pleasure for both of you, and reciprocity is not immediately required.

The second world, the one governed by market norms, is very different. There's nothing warm and fuzzy about it. The exchanges are sharp-edged: wages, prices, rents, interest, and costs-and-benefits. Such market relationships are not necessarily evil or mean—in fact, they also include self-reliance, inventiveness, and individualism—but they do imply comparable benefits and prompt payments. When you are in the domain of market norms, you get what you pay for—that's just the way it is.

When we keep social norms and market norms on their separate paths, life hums along pretty well. Take sex, for instance. We may have it free, in the social context, where it is, we hope, warm and emotionally nourishing. But there's also market sex, sex that is on demand and that costs money. This seems pretty straightforward. We don't have husbands (or wives) coming home asking for a $50 trick; nor do we have prostitutes hoping for everlasting love.

But when social and market norms collide, trouble sets in. Take sex again. A guy takes a girl out for dinner and a movie, and he pays the bills. They go out again, and he pays the bills once more. They go out a third time, and he's still springing for the meal and the entertainment. At this point, he's hoping for at least a passionate kiss at the front door. His wallet is getting perilously thin, but worse is what's going on in his head: he's having trouble reconciling the social norm (courtship) with the market norm (money for sex). On the fourth date he casually mentions how much this romance is costing him. Now he's crossed the line. Violation! She calls him a beast and storms off. He should have known that one can't mix social and market norms—especially in this case—without implying that the lady is a tramp. He should also have remembered the immortal words of Woody Allen: "The most expensive sex is free sex."

A FEW YEARS ago, James Heyman (a professor at the University of St. Thomas) and I decided to explore the effects of social and market norms. Simulating the Thanksgiving incident would have been wonderful, but considering the damage we might have done to our participants' family relationships, we chose something more mundane. In fact, it was one of the most boring tasks we could find (there is a tradition in social science of using very boring tasks).

In this experiment, a circle was presented on the left side of a computer screen and a box was presented on the right.

The task was to drag the circle, using the computer mouse, onto the square. Once the circle was successfully dragged to the square, it disappeared from the screen and a new circle appeared at the starting point. We asked the participants to drag as many circles as they could, and we measured how many circles they dragged within five minutes. This was our measure of their labor output—the effort that they would put into this task.

How could this setup shed light on social and market exchanges? Some of the participants received five dollars for participating in the short experiment. They were given the money as they walked into the lab; and they were told that at the end of the five minutes, the computer would alert them that the task was done, at which point they were to leave the lab. Because we paid them for their efforts, we expected them to apply market norms to this situation and act accordingly.

Participants in a second group were presented with the same basic instructions and task; but for them the reward was much lower (50 cents in one experiment and 10 cents in the other). Again we expected the participants to apply market norms to this situation and act accordingly.

Finally, we had a third group, to whom we introduced the tasks as a social request. We didn't offer the participants in this group anything concrete in return for their effort; it was merely a favor that we asked of them. We expected these participants to apply social norms to the situation and act accordingly.

How hard did the different groups work? In line with the ethos of market norms, those who received five dollars dragged on average 159 circles, and those who received 50 cents dragged on average 101 circles. As expected, more money caused our participants to be more motivated and work harder (by about 50 percent).

What about the condition with no money? Did these participants work less than the ones who got the low monetary payment—or, in the absence of money, did they apply social norms to the situation and work harder? The results showed that on average they dragged 168 circles, much more than those who were paid 50 cents, and just slightly more than those who were paid five dollars. In other words, our participants worked harder under the nonmonetary social norms than for the almighty buck (Ok, 50 cents).

Perhaps we should have anticipated this. There are many examples to show that people will work more for a cause than for cash. A few years ago, for instance, the AARP asked some lawyers if they would offer less expensive services to needy retirees, at something like $30 an hour. The lawyers said no. Then the program manager from AARP had a brilliant idea: he asked the lawyers if they would offer free services to needy retirees. Overwhelmingly, the lawyers said yes.

What was going on here? How could zero dollars be more attractive than $30? When money was mentioned, the lawyers used market norms and found the offer lacking, relative to their market salary. When no money was mentioned they used social norms and were willing to volunteer their time. Why didn't they just accept the $30, thinking of themselves as volunteers who received $30? Because once market norms enter our considerations, the social norms depart.

A similar lesson was learned by Nachum Sicherman, an economics professor at Columbia, who was taking martial arts lessons in Japan. The sensei (the master teacher) was not charging the group for the training. The students, feeling that this was unfair, approached the master one day and suggested that they pay him for his time and effort. Setting down his bamboo *shinai*, the master calmly replied that if he charged them, they would not be able to afford him.

IN THE PREVIOUS experiment, then, those who got paid 50 cents didn't say to themselves "Good for me; I get to do this favor for these researchers, and I am getting some money out of this," and continue to work harder than those who were paid nothing. Instead they switched themselves over to the market norms, decided that 50 cents wasn't much, and worked halfheartedly. In other words, when the market norms entered the lab, the social norms were pushed out.

But what would happen if we replaced the payments with a gift? Surely your mother-in-law would accept a good bottle of wine at dinner. Or how about a housewarming present (such as an eco-friendly plant) for a friend? Are gifts methods of exchange that keep us within the social exchange norms? Would participants receiving such gifts switch out of the social norms and into market norms, or would offering gifts as rewards maintain the participants in the social world?

To find out just where gifts fall on the line between social and market norms, James and I decided on a new experiment. This time, we didn't offer our participants money for dragging circles across a computer screen; we offered them gifts instead. We replaced the 50-cent reward with a Snickers bar (worth about 50 cents), and the five-dollar incentive with a box of Godiva chocolates (worth about five dollars).

The participants came to the lab, worked as much as they liked, and left. Then we looked at the results. As it turned out, all three experimental groups worked about equally hard during the task, regardless of whether they got a small Snickers bar (these participants dragged on average 162 circles), the Godiva chocolates (these participants dragged on average 169 circles), or nothing at all (these participants dragged on average 168 circles). The conclusion: no one is offended by a small gift, because even small gifts keep us in the social exchange world and away from market norms.

But what would happen if we mixed the signals for the two types of norms? What would happen if we blended the market norm with the social norm? In other words, if we said that we would give them a "50-*cent* Snickers bar" or a "*five-dollar* box of Godiva chocolates," what would the participants do? Would a "50-cent Snickers bar" make our participants work as hard as a "Snickers bar" made them work; or would it make them work halfheartedly, as the 50-cents made them work? Or would it be somewhere in the middle? The next experiment tested these ideas.

As it turned out, the participants were not motivated to work at all when they got the 50-cent Snickers bar, and in fact the effort they invested was the same as when they got a payment of 50 cents. They reacted to the explicitly priced gift in exactly the way they reacted to cash; and the gift no longer invoked social norms—it had passed into the realm of market norms.

By the way, we replicated the setup later when we asked passersby whether they would help us unload a sofa from a truck. We found the same results. People are willing to work for free, and they are willing to work for a reasonable wage; but offer them just a small payment and they will walk away. Gifts are also effective for sofas, and offering people a gift, even a small one, is sufficient to get them to help; but mention what the gift cost you, and you will see the back of them faster than you can say market norms.

THESE RESULTS SHOW that for market norms to emerge, it is sufficient to mention money (even when no money changes hands). But, of course, market norms are not just about effort—they relate to a broad range of behaviors including self-reliance, helping, and individualism. Would simply getting people to think about money influence them to behave differently in these respects? This premise was explored in a set of fantastic experiments by Kathleen Vohs (a professor at the University of Minnesota), Nicole Mead (a graduate student at Florida State University), and Miranda Goode (a graduate student at the University of British Columbia).

They asked the participants in their experiments to complete a "scrambled-sentence task," that is, to rearrange the order of words to form sentences. For the participants in one group, the task was based on neutral words (for example, "It's cold outside"); for the other group, the task was based on words related to money (for example "High-paying salary"*). Would thinking about money like this be sufficient to change the way participants behave?

In one of the experiments, the participants finished the unscrambling task and were then given a difficult puzzle, in which they had to arrange 12 disks into a square. As the experimenter left the room, he told them that they could come to him if they needed any help. Who do you think asked for help sooner—those who had worked on the "salary" sen-

---

*This general procedure is called priming, and the unscrambling task is used to get participants to think about a particular topic—without direct instructions to do so.

tences, with their implicit suggestion of money; or those who had worked on the "neutral" sentences, about the weather and other such topics? As it turned out, the students who had worked on the "salary" task struggled with the puzzle for about five and a half minutes before asking for help, whereas those who had worked on the neutral task asked for help after about three minutes. Thinking about money, then, made the participants in the "salary" group more self-reliant and less willing to ask for help.

But these participants were also less willing to help others. In fact, after thinking of money these participants were less willing to assist an experimenter enter data, less likely to help another participant who seemed confused, and less likely to help a "stranger" (an experimenter in disguise) who "accidentally" spilled a box of pencils.

Overall, the participants in the "salary" group showed many of the characteristics of the market: they were more selfish and self-reliant; they wanted to spend more time alone; they were more likely to select tasks that required individual input rather than teamwork; and when they were deciding where they wanted to sit, they chose seats farther away from whomever they were told to work with. Indeed, just thinking about money makes us behave as most economists believe we behave—and less like the social animals we are in our daily lives.

This leads me to a final thought: when you're in a restaurant with a date, for heaven's sake don't mention the price of the selections. Yes, they're printed clearly on the menu. Yes, this might be an opportunity to impress your date with the caliber of the restaurant. But if you rub it in, you'll be likely to shift your relationship from the social to the market norm. Yes, your date may fail to recognize how much this meal is setting you back. Yes, your mother-in-law may assume that the bottle of wine you've presented is a $10 blend, when it's a $60 special reserve merlot. That's the price you have to pay, though, to keep your relationships in the social domain and away from market norms.

SO WE LIVE in two worlds: one characterized by social exchanges and the other characterized by market exchanges. And we apply different norms to these two kinds of relationships. Moreover, introducing market norms into social exchanges, as we have seen, violates the social norms and hurts the relationships. Once this type of mistake has been committed, recovering a social relationship is difficult. Once you've offered to pay for the delightful Thanksgiving dinner, your mother-in-law will remember the incident for years to come. And if you've ever offered a potential romantic partner the chance to cut to the chase, split the cost of the courting process, and simply go to bed, the odds are that you will have wrecked the romance forever.

My good friends Uri Gneezy (a professor at the University of California at San Diego) and Aldo Rustichini (a professor at the University of Minnesota) provided a very clever test of the long-term effects of a switch from social to market norms.

A few years ago, they studied a day care center in Israel to determine whether imposing a fine on parents who arrived late to pick up their children was a useful deterrent. Uri and Aldo concluded that the fine didn't work well, and in fact it had long-term negative effects. Why? Before the fine was introduced, the teachers and parents had a social contract, with social norms about being late. Thus, if parents were late—as they occasionally were—they felt guilty, about it—and their guilt compelled them to be more prompt in picking up their kids in the future. (In Israel, guilt seems to be an effective way to get compliance.) But once the fine was imposed, the day care center had inadvertently replaced the social norms with market norms. Now that the parents were *paying* for their tardiness, they interpreted the situation in terms of market norms. In other words, since they were being fined, they could decide for themselves whether to be late or not. Needless to say, this was not what the daycare center intended.

BUT THE REAL story only started here. The most interesting part occurred a few weeks later, when the day care center removed the fine. Now the center was back to the social norm. Would the parents also return to the social norm? Would their guilt return as well? Not at all. Once the fine was removed, the behavior of the parents didn't change. They continued to pick up their kids late. In fact, when the fine was removed, there was a slight increase in the number of tardy pickups (after all, both the social and the market norms had been removed).

This experiment illustrates an unfortunate fact: when a social norm collides with a market norm, the social norm goes away. In other words, social relationships are not easy to reestablish. Once the bloom is off the rose—once a social norm is trumped by a market norm—it will rarely return.

THE FACT THAT we live in both the social world and the market world has many implications for our personal lives. From time to time, we all need someone to help us move something, or to watch our kids for a few hours, or to take in our mail when we're out of town. What's the best way to motivate our friends and neighbors to help us? Would cash do it—a gift, perhaps? How much? Or nothing at all? This social dance, as I'm sure you know, isn't easy to figure out—especially when there's a risk of pushing a relationship into the realm of a market exchange.

Here are some answers. Asking a friend to help move a large piece of furniture or a few boxes is fine. But asking a friend to help move a lot of boxes or furniture is not—especially if the friend is working side by side with movers who are getting paid for the same task. Your friend might begin to feel that he's being used. Similarly, asking your neighbor (who happens to be a lawyer) to bring in your mail while you're on vacation is fine. But asking him to spend the same amount of time preparing a rental contract for you—free—is not.

THE DELICATE BALANCE between social and market norms is also evident in the business world. In the last few decades companies have tried to market themselves as social companions—that is, they'd like us to think that they and we are family, or at least are friends who live on the same cul-de-sac. "Like a good neighbor, State Farm is there" is one familiar slogan. Another is Home Depot's gentle urging: "You can do it. We can help."

Whoever started the movement to treat customers socially had a great idea. If customers and a company are family, then the company gets several benefits. Loyalty is paramount. Minor infractions—screwing up your bill and even imposing a modest hike in your insurance rates—are accommodated.

Relationships of course have ups and downs, but overall they're a pretty good thing.

But here's what I find strange: although companies have poured billions of dollars into marketing and advertising to create social relationships—or at least an impression of social relationships—they don't seem to understand the nature of a social relationship, and in particular its risks.

For example, what happens when a customer's check bounces? If the relationship is based on market norms, the bank charges a fee, and the customer shakes it off. Business is business. While the fee is annoying, it's nonetheless acceptable. In a social relationship, however, a hefty late fee—rather than a friendly call from the manager or an automatic fee waiver—is not only a relationship-killer; it's a stab in the back. Consumers will take personal offense. They'll leave the bank angry and spend hours complaining to their friends about this awful bank. After all, this was a relationship framed as a social exchange. No matter how many cookies, slogans, and tokens of friendship a bank provides, one violation of the social exchange means that the consumer is back to the market exchange. It can happen that quickly.

What's the upshot? If you're a company, my advice is to remember that you can't have it both ways. You can't treat your customers like family one moment and then treat them impersonally—or, even worse, as a nuisance or a competitor—a moment later when this becomes more convenient or profitable. This is not how social relationships work. If you want a social relationship, go for it, but remember that you have to maintain it under all circumstances.

On the other hand, if you think you may have to play tough from time to time—charging extra for additional services or rapping knuckles swiftly to keep the consumers in line—you might not want to waste money in the first place on making your company the fuzzy feel-good choice. In that case, stick to a simple value proposition: state what you give and what you expect in return. Since you're not setting up any social norms or expectations, you also can't violate any—after all, it's just business.

COMPANIES HAVE ALSO tried to establish social norms with their employees. It wasn't always this way. Years ago, the workforce of America was more of an industrial, market-driven exchange. Back then it was often a nine-to-five, time-clock kind of mentality. You put in your 40 hours and you got your paycheck on Friday. Since workers were paid by the hour, they knew exactly when they were working for the man, and when they weren't. The factory whistle blew (or the corporate equivalent took place), and the transaction was finished. This was a clear market exchange, and it worked adequately for both sides.

Today companies see an advantage in creating a social exchange. After all, in today's market we're the makers of intangibles. Creativity counts more than industrial machines. The partition between work and leisure has likewise blurred. The people who ran the workplace want us to think about work while we're driving home and while we're in the shower. They've given us laptops, cell phones, and Blackberries to bridge the gap between the workplace and home.

Further blurring the nine-to-five workday is the trend in many companies to move away from hourly rates to monthly pay. In this 24/7 work environment social norms have a great advantage: they tend to make employees passionate, hard-working, flexible, and concerned. In a market where employees' loyalty to their employers is often wilting, social norms are one of the best ways to make workers loyal, as well as motivated.

Open-source software shows the potential of social norms. In the case of Linux and other collaborative projects, you can post a problem about a bug on one of the bulletin boards and see how fast someone, or often many people, will react to your request and fix the software—using their own leisure time. Could you pay for this level of service? Most likely. But if you had to hire people of the same caliber they would cost you an arm and a leg. Rather, people in these communities are happy to give their time to society at large (for which they get the same social benefits we all get from helping a friend paint a room). What can we learn from this that is applicable to the business world? There are other social rewards that strongly motivate behavior—and one of the least used in corporate life is the encouragement of social rewards and reputation.

If employees promise to work harder to achieve an important deadline (even canceling family obligations for it), if they are asked to get on an airplane at a moment's notice to attend a meeting, then they must get something similar in return—something like support when they are sick, or a chance to hold onto their jobs when the market threatens to take their jobs away.

BUT ALTHOUGH SOME companies have been successful in creating social norms with their workers, the current obsession with short-term profits, outsourcing, and draconian cost cutting threatens to undermine it all. In a social exchange, after all, people believe that if something goes awry the other party will be there for them, to protect and help them. These beliefs are not spelled out in a contract, but they are general obligations to provide care and help in times of need.

Again, companies cannot have it both ways. In particular, I am worried that the recent cuts we see in employees' benefits—child care, pensions, flextime, exercise rooms, the cafeteria, family picnics, etc.—are likely to come at the expense of the social exchange and thus affect workers' productivity. I am particularly worried that cuts in medical benefits are likely to transform much of the employer-employee social relationship to a market relationship.

If companies want to benefit from the advantages of social norms, they need to do a better job of cultivating those norms. Medical benefits, and in particular comprehensive medical coverage, are among the best ways a company can express its side of the social exchange. But what are many companies doing? They are demanding high deductibles in their insurance plans, and at the same time are reducing the scope of benefits. Simply put, they are undermining the social contract between the company and the employees and replacing it with market norms. As companies tilt the board, and employees slide from social norms to the realm of market norms, can we blame them for jumping ship when a better offer appears? It's really no surprise that "corporate loyalty," in terms of the loyalty of employees to their companies, has become an oxymoron.

Organizations can also think consciously about how people react to social and market norms. Should you give an employee a gift worth $1,000 or pay him or her $1,000 in cash? Which is better? If you ask the employees, the majority will most likely prefer cash over the gift. But the gift has its value, though this is sometimes ill understood—it can provide a boost to the social relationship between the employer and the employee, and by doing so provide long-term benefits to everyone. Think of it this way: who do you suppose is likely to work harder, show more loyalty, and truly love his work more—someone who is getting $1,000 in cash or someone who is getting a personal gift?

Of course, a gift is a symbolic gesture. And to be sure, no one is going to work for gifts rather than a salary. For that matter, no one is going to work for nothing. But if you look at companies like Google, which offers a wide variety of benefits for employees (including free gourmet lunches), you can see how much goodwill is created by emphasizing the social side of the company-worker relationship. It's remarkable how much work companies (particularly start-ups) can get out of people when social norms (such as the excitement of building something together) are stronger than market norms (such as salaries stepping up with each promotion).

If corporations started thinking in terms of social norms, in fact, they would realize that these norms build loyalty and—more important—make people want to extend themselves to the degree that corporations need today: to be flexible, concerned, and willing to pitch in. That's what a social relationship delivers.

THIS QUESTION OF social norms in the workplace is one we should be thinking about frequently. American's productivity depends increasingly on the talent and efforts of its workers. Could it be that we are driving business from the realm of social norms into market norms? Are workers thinking in terms of money, rather than the social values of loyalty and trust? What will that do to American productivity in the long run, in terms of creativity and commitment? And what of the "social contract" between government and the citizen? Is that at risk as well?

At some level we all know the answers. We understand, for instance, that people will not die for money. Police officers, firefighters, soldiers—they don't die for their weekly pay. It's the social norms—pride in their profession and a sense of duty—that will motivate them to give up their lives and health. A friend of mine in Miami once accompanied a U.S. customs agent on a patrol of the offshore waters. The agent carried an AK-47 rifle and could certainly have pounded several holes into a fleeing drug boat. But had he ever done so? No way, he replied. He wasn't about to get himself killed for the government salary he received. In fact, he confided, his group had an unspoken agreement with the drug couriers: the feds wouldn't fire if the drug dealers didn't fire. (Perhaps that's why we rarely (if ever) hear about gun battles on the edges of America's "war on drugs.")

How could we change this situation? First, we could make the federal salary so good that the customs agent would be willing to risk his life for it. But how much money is that? Compensation equal to what the typical drug trafficker gets for racing a boat from the Bahamas to Miami? Alternatively, we could elevate the social norm, making the officer feel that his mission is worth more than his base pay—that we honor him (as we honor our police and firefighters) for a job which not only stabilizes the structure of society but also saves our kids from all kinds of dangers. That would take some inspirational leadership, of course, but it could be done.

Let me describe how that same thought applies to the world of education. I recently joined a federal committee on incentives and accountability in public education. This is one aspect of social and market norms that I would like to explore in the years to come. Our task is reexamine the "No Child Left Behind" policy, and to help find ways to motivate students, teachers, administrators, and parents.

My feeling so far is that standardized testing and performance-based salaries are likely to push education from social norms to market norms. The United States already spends more money per student than any other western society. Would it be wise to add more money? The same consideration applies to for testing: we are already testing very frequently, and more testing is unlikely to improve the quality of education.

I suspect that one answer lies in the realm of social norms. As we learned in our experiments, cash will take you only so far—but social norms are the forces that can make a difference in the long run. Instead of focusing the attention of the teachers, parents, and kids on test scores, salaries, and competition, it might be better to instill in all of us a sense of purpose, mission, and pride in education. To do this we certainly can't take the path of market norms. The Beatles proclaimed some time ago that you "Can't Buy Me Love" and this also applies to the love of learning—you can't buy it; and if you try, you might chase it away.

So how can we improve the educational system? We should probably first rethink school curricula, and link them in more obvious ways to social goals (elimination of poverty and crime, elevation of human rights, etc.), technological goals (boosting energy conservation, space exploration, nanotechnology, etc.), and medical goals (cures for cancer, diabetes, obesity, etc.) that we care about as a society. This way the students, teachers, and parents might see the larger point in education and become more enthusiastic and motivated about it. We should also work hard on making education a goal in itself, and stop confusing the number of hours students spend in school with the quality of the education they get. Kids can get excited about many things (baseball, for example), and it is our challenge as a society to make them want to know as much about Nobel laureates as they now know about baseball players. I am not suggesting that igniting a social passion for education is simple; but if we are successful in doing so, the value could be immense.

MONEY, AS IT turns out, is very often the most expensive way to motivate people. Social norms are not only cheaper, but often more effective as well.

So what good is money? In ancient times, money made trading easier: you didn't have to sling a goose over your back when you went to market, or decide what section of the goose was equivalent to a head of lettuce. In modern times money has even more benefits, as it allows us to specialize, borrow, and save.

But money has also taken on a life of its own. As we have seen, it can remove the best in human interactions. So do we need money? Of course we do, but could there be some aspects of our life that would be in some ways better without it?

That's a radical idea, and not an easy one to imagine. But a few years ago I had a taste of it. At that time, I got a phone call from John Perry Barlow, a former lyricist for the Grateful Dead, inviting me to an event that proved to be both an important personal experience and an interesting exercise in creating a moneyless society. Barlow told me that I had to come to Burning Man with him, and that if I did, I would feel as if I had come home. Burning Man is an annual week-long event of self-expression and self-reliance held in Black Rock Desert, Nevada, regularly attended by more than 40,000 people. Burning Man started in 1986 on Baker Beach in San Francisco, when a small crowd designed, built, and eventually set fire to an eight-foot wooden statue of a man and a smaller wooden dog. Since then the size of the man being burned and the number of people who attend the festivities has grown considerably, and the event is now one of the largest art festivals, and an ongoing experiment in temporary community.

Burning Man has many extraordinary aspects, but for me one of the most remarkable is its rejection of market norms. Money is not accepted anywhere at Burning Man. Rather, the whole place works as a gift exchange economy—you give things to other people, with the understanding that they will give something back to you (or to someone else at some point in the future). Thus, people who can cook might fix a meal. Psychologists offer free counseling sessions. Masseuses massage those lying on tables before them. Those who have water offer showers. People give away drinks, homemade jewelry, and hugs. (I made some puzzles at the hobby shop at MIT, and gave them to people. Mostly, people enjoyed trying to solve them.)

At first this was all very strange, but before long I found myself adopting the norms of Burning Man. I was surprised, in fact, to find that Burning Man was the most accepting, social, and caring place I had ever been. I'm not sure I could easily survive in Burning Man for all 52 weeks of the year. But this experience has convinced me that life with fewer market norms and more social norms would be more satisfying, creative, fulfilling, and fun.

The answer, I believe, is not to re-create society as Burning Man, but to remember that social norms can play a far greater role in society than we have been giving them credit for. In fact, if we contemplate how market norms have gradually taken over our lives in the past few decades—with their emphasis on higher salaries, more income, and more spending—we may recognize that a return to some of the old social norms might not be so bad after all. In fact, it might bring quite a bit of the old civility back to our lives.

CHAPTER 5

The Influence of Arousal

Why Hot Is Much Hotter Than We Realize

Ask most twentysomething male college students whether they would ever attempt unprotected sex and they will quickly recite chapter and verse about the risk of dreaded diseases and pregnancy. Ask them in any dispassionate circumstances—while they are doing homework or listening to a lecture—whether they'd enjoy being spanked, or enjoy sex in a threesome with another man, and they'll wince. No way, they'd tell you. Furthermore, they'd narrow their eyes at you and think, What kind of sicko are you anyhow, asking these questions in the first place?

In 2001, while I was visiting Berkeley for the year, my friend, academic hero, and longtime collaborator George Loewenstein and I invited a few bright students to help us understand the degree to which rational, intelligent people can predict how their attitudes will change when they are in an impassioned state. In order to make this study realistic, we needed to measure the participants' responses while they were smack in the midst of such an emotional state. We could have made our participants feel angry or hungry, frustrated or annoyed. But we preferred to have them experience a pleasurable emotion.

We chose to study decision making under sexual arousal—not because we had kinky predilections ourselves, but because it might help society grapple with some of its most difficult problems, such as teen pregnancy and the spread of HIV-AIDS. There are sexual motivations everywhere we look, and yet we understand very little about how these influence our decision making.

Moreover, since we wanted to understand whether participants would be able to predict how they would behave in a particular emotional state, the emotion needed to be one that was already quite familiar to them. That made our decision easy. If there's anything predictable and familiar about twentysomething male college students, it's the regularity with which they think about sex.

ROY, AN AFFABLE, studious biology major at Berkeley, is in a sweat—and not over finals. Propped up in the single bed of his darkened dorm room, he's masturbating rapidly with his right hand. With his left, he's using a one-handed keyboard to manipulate a Saran-wrapped laptop computer. As he idles through pictures of buxom naked women lolling around in various erotic poses, his heart pounds ever more loudly in his chest.

As he becomes increasingly excited, Roy adjusts the "arousal meter" on the computer screen upward. As he reaches the bright red "high" zone, a question pops up on the screen:

Could you enjoy sex with someone you hated?

Roy moves his left hand to a scale that ranges from "no" to "yes" and taps his answer. The next question appears: "Would you slip a woman a drug to increase the chance that she would have sex with you?"

Again, Roy selects his answer, and a new question pops up. "Would you always use a condom?"

BERKELEY ITSELF IS a dichotomous place. It was a site of antiestablishment riots in the 1960s, and people in the Bay Area snarkily refer to the famously left-of-center city as the "People's Republic of Berkeley." But the large campus itself draws a surprisingly conformist population of top-level students. In a survey of incoming freshmen in 2004, only 51.2 percent of the respondents thought of themselves as liberal. More than one-third (36 percent) deemed their views middle-of-the-road, and 12 percent claimed to be conservatives. To my surprise, when I arrived at Berkeley, I found that the students were in general not very wild, rebellious, or likely to take risks.

The ads we posted around Sproul Plaza read as follows: "Wanted: Male research participants, heterosexual, 18 years-plus, for a study on decision making and arousal." The ad noted that the experimental sessions would demand about an hour of the participants' time, that the participants would be paid $10 per session, and that the experiments could involve sexually arousing material. Those interested in applying could respond to Mike, the research assistant, by e-mail.

For this study, we decided to seek out only men. In terms of sex, their wiring is a lot simpler than that of women (as we concluded after much discussion among ourselves and our assistants, both male and female). A copy of *Playboy* and a darkened room was about all we'd need for a high degree of success.

Another concern was getting the project approved at the MIT Sloan School of Management (where I had my primary appointment). This was an ordeal in itself. Before allowing the research to begin, Dean Richard Schmalensee assigned a committee, consisting mostly of women, to examine the project. This committee had several concerns. What if a participant uncovered repressed memories of sexual abuse as a result of the research? Suppose a participant found that he or she was a sex addict? Their questions seemed unwarranted to me, since any college student with a computer and an Internet connection can get hold of the most graphic pornography imaginable.

Although the business school was stymied by this, I was fortunate to have a position at MIT's media lab as well, and Walter Bender, who was the head of the lab, happily approved the project. I was on my way. But my experience with MIT's Sloan School made it clear that even half a century after Kinsey, sex is still largely a taboo subject for a study—at least at some business schools.

In any case, our ads went out; and, college men being what they are, we soon had a long list of hearty fellows awaiting the chance to participate—including Roy.

Roy, in fact, was typical of most of the 25 participants in our study. Born and raised in San Francisco, he was accomplished, intelligent, and kind—the kind of kid every prospective mother-in-law dreams of. Roy played Chopin études on the piano and liked to dance to techno music. He had earned straight A's throughout high school, where he was captain of the varsity volleyball team. He sympathized with libertarians and tended to vote Republican. Friendly and affable, he had a steady girlfriend who he'd been dating for a year. He planned to go to medical school and had a weakness for spicy California-roll sushi and for the salads at Cafe Intermezzo.

Roy met with our graduate student research assistant, Mike, at Strada coffee shop—Berkeley's patio-style percolator for many an intellectual thought, including the idea for the solution to Fermat's last theorem. Mike was slender and tall, with short hair, an artistic air, and an engaging smile.

Mike shook hands with Roy, and they sat down. "Thanks for answering our ad, Roy," Mike said, pulling out a few sheets of paper and placing them on the table. "First, let's go over the consent forms."

Mike intoned the ritual decree: The study was about decision making and sexual arousal. Participation was voluntary. Data would be confidential. Participants had the right to contact the committee in charge of protecting the rights of those participating in experiments, and so on.

Roy nodded and nodded. You couldn't find a more agreeable participant.

"You can stop the experiment at any time," Mike concluded. "Everything understood?"

"Yes," Roy said. He grabbed a pen and signed. Mike shook his hand.

"Great!" Mike took a cloth bag out of his knapsack. "Here's what's going to happen." He unwrapped an Apple iBook computer and opened it up. In addition to the standard keyboard, Roy saw a 12-key multicolored keypad.

"It's a specially equipped computer," Mike explained. "Please use only this keypad to respond." He touched the keys on the colored pad. "We'll give you a code to enter, and this code will let you start the experiment. During the session, you'll be asked a series of questions to which you can answer on a scale ranging between 'no' and 'yes.' If you think you would like the activity described in the question, answer 'yes,' and if you think you would not, answer 'no.' Remember that you're being asked to predict how you would behave and what kind of activities you would like when aroused."

Roy nodded.

"We'll ask you to sit in your bed, and set the computer up on a chair on the left side of your bed, in clear sight and reach of your bed," Mike went on. "Place the keypad next to you so that you can use it without any difficulty, and be sure you're alone."

Roy's eyes twinkled a little.

"When you finish with the session, write to me and we will meet again, and you'll get your ten bucks."

Mike didn't tell Roy about the questions themselves. The session started by asking Roy to imagine that he was sexually aroused, and to answer all the questions as he would if he were aroused. One set of questions asked about about sexual preferences. Would he, for example, find women's shoes erotic? Could he imagine being attracted to a 50-year-old woman? Could it be fun to have sex with someone who was extremely fat? Could having sex with someone he hated be enjoyable? Would it be fun to get tied up or to tie someone else up? Could "just kissing" be frustrating?

A second set of questions asked about the likelihood of engaging in immoral behaviors such as date rape. Would Roy tell a woman that he loved her to increase the chance that she would have sex with him? Would he encourage a date to drink to increase the chance that she would have sex with him? Would he keep trying to have sex after a date had said "no"?

A third set of questions asked about Roy's likelihood of engaging in behaviors related to unsafe sex. Does a condom decrease sexual pleasure? Would he always use a condom if he didn't know the sexual history of a new sexual partner? Would he use a condom even if he was afraid that a woman might change her mind while he went to get it?*

A few days later, having answered the questions in his "cold," rational state, Roy met again with Mike.

"Those were some interesting questions," Roy noted.

"Yes, I know," Mike said coolly. "Kinsey had nothing on us. By the way, we have another set of experimental sessions. Would you be interested in participating again?"

Roy smiled a little, shrugged, and nodded.

Mike shoved a few pages toward him. "This time we're asking you to sign the same consent form, but the next task will be slightly different. The next session will be very much the same as the last one, but this time we want you to get yourself into an excited state by viewing a set of arousing pictures and masturbating. What we want you to do is arouse yourself to a high level, but not to ejaculate. In case you do, though, the computer will be protected."

Mike pulled out the Apple iBook. This time the keyboard and the screen were covered with a thin layer of Saran wrap.

Roy made a face. "I didn't know computers could get pregnant."

"Not a chance," Mike laughed. "This one had its tubes tied. But we like to keep them clean."

Mike explained that Roy would browse through a series

---

*For a complete lists of the questions we asked, see the appendix to this chapter.

of erotic pictures on the computer to help him get to the right level of arousal; then he would answer the same questions as before.

WITHIN THREE MONTHS, some fine Berkeley undergraduate students had undergone a variety of sessions in different orders. In the set of sessions conducted when they were in a cold, dispassionate state, they predicted what their sexual and moral decisions would be if they were aroused. In the set of sessions conducted when they were in a hot, aroused state, they also predicted their decisions—but this time, since they were actually in the grip of passion, they were presumably more aware of their preferences in that state. When the study was completed, the conclusions were consistent and clear—overwhelmingly clear, frighteningly clear.

In every case, our bright young participants answered the questions very differently when they were aroused and when they were in the "cold" state. Across the 19 questions about sexual preferences, when Roy and all the other participants were aroused they predicted that their desire to engage in a variety of somewhat odd sexual activities would be nearly twice as high as (72 percent higher) they had predicted when they were "cold." For example, the idea of enjoying contact with animals was more than twice as appealing when they were in a state of arousal as when they were in a "cold" state. In the five questions about their propensity to engage in immoral activities, when they were aroused they predicted their propensity to be more than twice as high as (136 percent higher) they had predicted in the cold state. Similarly, in the set of questions about using condoms, and despite the warnings that had been hammered into them over the years about the importance of condoms, they were more likely in the aroused state than in the cold state (the proportion was 25 percent higher) to predict that they would forgo condoms. Again, they failed to predict the influence of arousal on their approach to safe sex.

The results showed that when Roy and the other participants were in a cold, rational, superego-driven state, they respected women; they were not particularly attracted to the odd sexual activities we asked them about; they always took the moral high ground; and they expected that they would always use a condom. They thought that they understood themselves, their preferences, and what actions they were capable of. But as it turned out, they completely underestimated their reactions.

No matter how we looked at the numbers, it was clear that the magnitude of underprediction by the participants was substantial. Across the board, they revealed in their aroused state that they themselves did not know what they were like when aroused. Prevention, protection, conservatism, and morality were nowhere on the radar screen. They were unable to predict the degree to which passion would change them.*

IMAGINE WAKING UP one morning, looking in the mirror, and discovering that someone else—something alien but human—has taken over your body. You're uglier, shorter, hairier; your lips are thinner, your incisors are longer, your nails are filthy, your face is flatter. Two cold, reptilian eyes

---

*These results apply most directly to sexual arousal and its influence on who we are; but we can also assume that other emotional states (anger, hunger, excitement, jealousy, and so on) work in similar ways, making us strangers to ourselves.

gaze back at you. You long to smash something, rape someone. You are not you. You are a monster.

Beset by this nightmarish vision, Robert Louis Stevenson
screamed in his sleep in the early hours of an autumn morning in 1885. Immediately after his wife awoke him, he set to
work on what he called a "fine bogey tale"—*Dr. Jekyll and
Mr. Hyde*—in which he said, "Man is not truly one, but truly
two." The book was an overnight hit, and no wonder. The
story captivated the imagination of Victorians, who were fas-
cinated with the dichotomy between repressive propriety—
represented by the mild-mannered scientist Dr. Jekyll—and
uncontrollable passion, embodied in the murderous Mr.
Hyde. Dr. Jekyll thought he understood how to control himself. But when Mr. Hyde took over, look out.

The story was frightening and imaginative, but it wasn't
new. We all know that human beings operate differently in
rational and irrational states. Long before Sophocles's *Oedi-
pus Rex* and Shakespeare's *Macbeth*, the war between interior good and evil had been the stuff of myth, religion, and
literature. In Freudian terms, each of us houses a dark self,
an id, a brute that can unpredictably wrest controls away
from the superego. Thus a pleasant, friendly neighbor, seized
by road rage, crashes his car into a semi. A teenager grabs a
gun and shoots his friends. A priest rapes a boy. All these
otherwise good people assume that they understand themselves. But in the heat of passion, suddenly, with the flip of
some interior switch, everything changes.

Our experiment at Berkeley revealed not just the old story
that we are all like Jekyll and Hyde, but also something
new—that every one of us, regardless of how "good" we are,
underpredicts the effect of passion on our behavior. In every
case, the participants in our experiment got it wrong. Even

the most brilliant and rational person, in the heat of passion, seems to be absolutely and completely divorced from the person he thought he was. Moreover, it is not just that people make wrong predictions about themselves—their predictions are wrong by a large margin.

Most of the time, according to the results of the study, Roy is smart, decent, reasonable, kind, and trustworthy. His frontal lobes are fully functioning; his executive is functioning to control his behavior. But when he's in a state of sexual arousal and the reptilian brain takes over, he becomes unrecognizable to himself.

Roy thinks he knows how he will behave in an aroused state, but his understanding is limited. He doesn't know that as his sexual motivators become more intense and varied, he may throw caution to the wind. He may risk sexually transmitted diseases and unwanted pregnancies in order to achieve sexual gratification. When he is gripped by passion, his emotions may blur the boundary between what is right and wrong. In fact, he doesn't have a clue to how consistently wild he really is, for when he is in one state and tries to predict his behavior in another state, he may get it wrong.

Moreover, the study suggested that our inability to understand ourselves in a different emotional state does not seem to improve with experience, even if we spend as much time in this state as our Berkeley students spend sexually aroused. Sexual arousal is familiar, personal, very human, and utterly commonplace. Even so, we all systematically underpredict the degree to which arousal completely negates our superego, and the way emotions can take control of our behavior.

WHAT HAPPENS, THEN, when our irrational self comes alive

in an emotional place that we think is familiar but in fact is unfamiliar? If we fail to really understand ourselves, is it possible to somehow predict how we or others will behave when "out of our heads"—when we're really angry, hungry, frightened or sexually aroused? Is it possible to do something about this?

The answers to these questions are profound, for they indicate that we must be wary of situations in which our Mr. Hyde may take over. When the boss criticizes us publicly, we might be tempted to respond with a vehement e-mail. But wouldn't we be better off putting our reply in the "draft" folder for a few days? When we are smitten by a sports car after a test-drive with the wind in our hair, shouldn't we take a break—and discuss our spouse's plan to buy a minivan— before signing a contract to buy the car?

Here are a few more examples of ways to protect ourselves from ourselves:

Safe Sex

Many parents and teenagers, while in a cold, rational, Dr. Jekyll state, tend to believe that the mere promise of abstinence—commonly known as "Just say no"—is sufficient protection against sexually transmitted diseases and unwanted pregnancies. Assuming that this thought will prevail even when emotions reach the boiling point, the advocates of "just saying no" see no reason to carry a condom with them. But as our study shows, in the heat of passion, we are all in danger of switching from "Just say no" to "Yes!" in a heartbeat; and if no condom is available, we are likely to say yes, regardless of the dangers.

What does this suggest? First, widespread availability of

condoms is essential. We should not decide in a cool state whether or not to bring condoms; they must be there just in case. Second, unless students start to understand how they might react in an emotional state, they will not be able to predict this. Thus sex education should focus less on the physiology and biology of the reproductive system, and more on strategies to deal with the emotions that accompany sexual arousal. Third, we must admit that carrying condoms and even vaguely understanding the emotional firestorm of sexual arousal may not be enough.

There are most likely many situations where teenagers simply won't be able to cope with their emotions. A better strategy, for those who want to guarantee that teenagers avoid sex, is to teach teenagers that they must walk away from the fire of passion before they are close enough to be drawn in. Accepting this advice might not be easy, but our results suggest that it is easier for them to fight temptation before it arises than after it has started to lure them in. In other words, avoiding temptation altogether is easier than fighting it.

To be sure, this sounds a lot like the "Just say no" campaign, which urges teenagers to walk away from sex when tempted. But the difference is that "Just say no" assumes we can turn off passion at will, at any point, whereas our study shows this assumption to be false. If we put aside the debate on the pros and cons of teenage sex, what is clear is that if we want to help teenagers avoid sex, sexually transmitted diseases, and unwanted pregnancies, we have two strategies. Either we can teach them how to say no *before* any temptation takes hold, and before a situation becomes impossible to resist; or alternatively, we can get them prepared to deal with the consequences of saying yes in the heat of passion (by carrying a condom, for example). One thing is sure: if we don't teach our young people how to deal with sex when they are half out of their minds, we are not only fooling them; we're fooling ourselves as well. Whatever lessons we teach them, we need to help them understand that they will react differently when they are calm and cool from when their hormones are raging at fever pitch (and of course the same also applies to our own behavior).

Safe Driving

Similarly, we need to teach teenagers (and everyone else) not to drive when their emotions are at a boil. It's not just inexperience and hormones that make so many teenagers crash their own or their parents' cars. It's also the ear full of laughing friends, with the CD player blaring at an adrenaline-pumping decibel level, and the driver's right hand searching for the french fries or his girlfriend's knee. Who's thinking about risk in that situation? Probably no one. A recent study found that a teenager driving alone was 40 percent more likely to get into an accident than an adult. But with one other teenager in the car, the percentage was twice that—and with a third teenager along for the ride, the percentage doubled again.[6]

To react to this, we need an intervention that does not rely on the premise that teenagers will remember how they wanted to behave when in a cold state (or how their parents wanted them to behave) and follow these guidelines. Why not build into cars precautionary devices to foil teenagers' behavior? Such cars might be equipped with a modified Onstar system that the teenager and the parents configure in a "cold" state. If a car exceeds 65 miles per hour on the highway, or more than 40 miles per hour in a residential zone, for example, there will be consequences. If the car exceeds the speed limit or begins to make erratic turns, the radio might switch from 2pac to Schumann's Second Symphony (this would slow most teenagers). Or the car might blast the air conditioning in winter, switch on the heat in summer, or automatically call Mom (a real downer if the driver's friends are present). By then, the driver and his or her friends would realize that it's time for Mr. Hyde to move over and let Dr. Jekyll drive.

This is not at all far-fetched. Modern cars are already full of computers that control the fuel injection, the climate system, and the sound system. Cars equipped with Onstar are already linked to a wireless network. With today's technology, it would be a simple matter for a car to automatically call Mom.

Better Life Decisions

Not uncommonly, women who are pregnant for the first time tell their doctors, before to the onset of labor, that they will refuse any kind of painkiller. The decision made in their cold state is admirable, but they can't imagine the pain that can come with childbirth (let alone the challenges of child rearing). After all is said and done, they may wish they'd gone for the epidural.

With this in mind, Sumi (my lovely wife) and I, readying ourselves for the birth of our first child, decided to test our mettle before making any decisions about using an epidural. To do this, Sumi plunged her hands into a bucket of ice for two minutes (we did this on the advice of our birth coach, who swore to us that the resulting pain would be similar to the pain of childbirth), while I coached her breathing. If Sumi was unable to bear the pain of this experience, we figured, she'd probably want painkillers when she was going through the actual birth. After two minutes of holding her hands in the ice bucket, Sumi clearly understood the appeal of an epidural. During the birth itself, any ounce of love she ever had for her husband was completely transferred to the anesthesiologist, who produced the epidural at the critical point. (With our second child, we made it to the hospital about two minutes before Neta was born, so Sumi did end up experiencing an analgesic-free birth after all.)

LOOKING FROM ONE emotional state to another is difficult. It's not always possible; and as Sumi learned it can quite often be painful. But to make informed decisions we need to somehow experience and understand the emotional state we will be in at the other side of the experience. Learning how to bridge this gap is essential to making some of the important decisions of our lives.

It is unlikely that we would move to a different city without asking friends who live there how they like it, or even choose to see a film without reading some reviews. Isn't it strange that we invest so little in learning about both sides of our emotions? Why should we reserve this subject for psychology classes when the failure to understand it can bring about repeated failures in many aspects of our lives? We need to explore the two sides of ourselves; we need to understand the cold state and the hot state; we need to see how the gap between the hot and cold states benefits our lives, and where it leads us astray.

What did our experiments suggest? It may be that our models of human behavior need to be rethought. There is no such thing as a fully integrated human being. We may, in fact, be an agglomeration of multiple selves. Although there is nothing much we can do to get our Dr. Jekyll to fully appreciate the strength of our Mr. Hyde, perhaps just being aware that we are prone to making the wrong decisions when gripped by intense emotion may help us, in some way, to apply our knowledge of our "Hyde" selves to our daily activities.

In Chapter 6, I will explain this idea a bit more.

APPENDIX: CHAPTER 5

A complete list of the questions we asked, with the mean response and percentage differences. Each question was presented on a visual-analog scale that stretched between "no" on the left (zero) to "possibly" in the middle (50) to "yes" on the right (100).

TABLE 1
RATE THE ATTRACTIVENESS OF DIFFERENT ACTIVITIES

Question	Nonaroused	Aroused	Difference, percent
Are women's shoes erotic?	42	65	55
Can you imagine being attracted to a 12-year-old girl?	23	46	100
Can you imagine having sex with a 40-year-old woman?	58	77	33
Can you imagine having sex with a 50-year-old woman?	28	55	96
Can you imagine having sex with a 60-year-old woman?	7	23	229
Can you imagine having sex with a man?	8	14	75
Could it be fun to have sex with someone who was extremely fat?	13	24	85
Could you enjoy having sex with someone you hated?	53	77	45
If you were attracted to a woman and she proposed a threesome with a man, would you do it?	19	34	79
Is a woman sexy when she's sweating?	56	72	29
Is the smell of cigarette smoke arousing?	13	22	69
Would it be fun to get tied up by your sexual partner?	63	81	29
Would it be fun to tie up your sexual partner?	47	75	60
Would it be fun to watch an attractive woman urinating?	25	32	28
Would you find it exciting to spank your sexual partner?	61	72	18
Would you find it exciting to get spanked by an attractive woman?	50	68	36
Would you find it exciting to have anal sex?	46	77	67
Can you imagine getting sexually excited by contact with an animal?	6	16	167
Is just kissing frustrating?	41	69	68

RATE THE LIKELIHOOD OF ENGAGING IN IMMORAL BEHAVIORS LIKE DATE RAPE (A STRICT ORDER OF SEVERITY IS NOT IMPLIED)

Question	Nonaroused	Aroused	Difference, percent
Would you take a date to a fancy restaurant to increase your chance of having sex with her?	55	70	27
Would you tell a woman that you loved her to increase the chance that she would have sex with you?	30	51	70
Would you encourage your date to drink to increase the chance that she would have sex with you?	46	63	37
Would you keep trying to have sex after your date says "no"?	20	45	125
Would you slip a woman a drug to increase the chance that she would have sex with you?	5	26	420

TABLE 3
RATE YOUR TENDENCY TO USE, AND OUTCOMES OF NOT USING, BIRTH CONTROL

Question	Nonaroused	Aroused	Difference, percent
Birth control is the woman's responsibility.	34	44	29
A condom decreases sexual pleasure.	66	78	18
A condom interferes with sexual spontaneity.	58	73	26
Would you always use a condom if you didn't know the sexual history of a new sexual partner?	88	69	22
Would you use a condom even if you were afraid that a woman might change her mind while you went to get it?	86	60	30

CHAPTER 6

The Problem of Procrastination and Self-Control

Why We Can't Make Ourselves Do What We Want to Do

Onto the American scene, populated by big homes, big cars, and big-screen plasma televisions, comes another big phenomenon: the biggest decline in the personal savings rate since the Great Depression.

Go back 25 years, and double-digit savings rates were the norm. As recently as 1994 the savings rate was nearly five percent. But by 2006 the savings rate had fallen below zero—to negative one percent. Americans were not only not saving; they were spending more than they earned. Europeans do a lot better—they save an average of 20 percent. Japan's rate is 25 percent. China's is 50 percent. So what's up with America?

I suppose one answer is that Americans have succumbed to rampant consumerism. Go back to a home built before we had to have everything, for instance, and check out the size of the closets. Our house in Cambridge, Massachusetts, for example, was built in 1890. It has no closets whatsoever. Houses in the 1940s had closets barely big enough to stand in. The closet of the 1970s was a bit larger, perhaps deep enough for a fondue pot, a box of eight-track tapes, and a few disco dresses. But the closet of today is a different breed. "Walk-in closet" means that you can literally walk in for quite a distance. And no matter how deep these closets are, Americans have found a way to fill it them right up to the closet door.

Another answer—the other half of the problem—is the recent explosion in consumer credit. The average American family now has six credit cards (in 2005 alone, Americans received 6 billion direct-mail solicitations for credit cards). Frighteningly, the average family debt on these cards is about $9,000; and even in 10 households borrow on credit cards to cover such basic living expenses as food, utilities, and clothing.

So wouldn't it just be wiser if Americans learned to save, as in the old days, and as the rest of the world does, by diverting some cash to the cookie jar, and delaying some purchases until we can really afford them? Why can't we save part of our paychecks, as we know we should? Why can't we resist those new purchases? Why can't we exert some good old-fashioned self-control?

The road to hell, they say, is paved with good intentions. And most of us know what that's all about. We promise to save for retirement, but we spend the money on a vacation. We vow to diet, but we surrender to the allure of the dessert cart. We promise to have our cholesterol checked regularly, and then we cancel our appointment.

How much do we lose when our fleeting impulses deflect us from our long-term goals? How much is our health affected by those missed appointments and our lack of exercise? How much is our wealth reduced when we forget our vow to save more and consume less? Why do we lose the fight against procrastination so frequently?

IN THE LAST Chapter we discussed how emotions grab hold of us and make us view the world from a different perspective. Procrastination (from the Latin *pro*, meaning *for*; and *cras*, meaning *tomorrow*) is rooted in the same kind of problem. When we promise to save our money, we are in a cool state. When we promise to exercise and watch our diet, again we're cool. But then the lava flow of hot emotion comes rushing in: just when we promise to save, we see a new car, a mountain bike or a pair of shoes that we must have. Just when we plan to exercise regularly, we find a reason to sit all day in front of the television. And as for the diet? I'll take that slice of chocolate cake, and begin the diet in earnest tomorrow. Giving up on our long-term goals for immediate gratification, my friends, is procrastination.

As a university professor, I'm all too familiar with procrastination. At the beginning of every semester my students make heroic promises to themselves—vowing to read their assignments on time, submit their papers on time, and in general, stay on top of things. And every semester I've watched as temptation takes them out on a date, over to the student union for a meeting, and off on a ski trip in the mountains—while their workload falls farther and farther behind. In the end, they wind up impressing me, not with their punctuality, but with their creativity—inventing stories, excuses, and family tragedies to explain their tardiness. (Why do family tragedies generally occur in the last two weeks of the semester?)

After I'd been teaching at MIT for a few years, my colleague Klaus Wertenbroch (a professor at INSEAD, a business school based in Paris) and I decided to work up a few studies that might get to the root of the problem, and just maybe offer a fix for this common human weakness. Our guinea pigs this time would be the delightful students in my class on consumer behavior.

As they settled into their chairs that first morning, full of anticipation (and, no doubt, early resolutions to stay on top of their class assignments), the students listened to me review the syllabus for the course. There would be three main papers over the 12-week semester, I explained. Together, these papers would constitute much of their final grade.

"And what are the deadlines?" asked one of them, waving his hand from the back. I smiled. "You can hand in the papers at any time before the end of the semester," I replied. "It's entirely up to you." The students looked back blankly.

"Here's the deal," I explained. "By the end of the week, you must commit to a deadline date for each paper. Once you set your deadlines, they can't be changed." Late papers, I explained, would be penalized at the rate of one percent off the grade for each day late. The students could always turn in their papers before their deadlines, of course, but since I wouldn't be reading any of them until the end of the semester, there would be no particular advantage in terms of grades for doing so.

In other words, the ball was in their court. Would they have the self-control to play the game?

"But Professor Ariely," asked Gurev, a clever master's student with a charming Indian accent, "given these instructions and incentives, wouldn't it make sense for us to select the last date possible?"

"You can do that," I replied. "If you find that it makes sense, by all means do it."

Under these conditions, what would you have done?

I promise to submit paper 1 on week ———
I promise to submit paper 2 on week ———
I promise to submit paper 3 on week ———

What deadlines did the students pick for themselves? A perfectly rational student would follow Gurev's advice and set all the deadlines at the last day of class—after all it was always possible to submit papers earlier without a penalty, so why take a chance and select an earlier deadline than needed? Delaying the deadlines to the end was clearly the best decision if students were perfectly rational. But what if the students are not rational? What if they succumb to temptation and are prone to procrastination? What if they realize their weakness? If the students are not rational, and they know it, they could use the deadlines to force themselves to behave better. They could set early deadlines and by doing so force themselves to start working on the projects earlier in the semester.

What did my students do? They used the scheduling tool I provided them with, and they spaced the timing of their papers across the whole semester. This is fine and good, as it suggests that the students realize their problems with procrastination and that if given the right opportunities they try to control themselves—but the main question is whether the tool was indeed helpful in improving their grades. To find out about this, we had to conduct other versions of the same experiments in other classes and compare the grades for the papers.

Now THAT I had Gurev and his classmates choosing their individual deadlines, I went to my other two classes—with markedly different deals. In the second class, I told the students that they would have no deadlines at all during the semester. They merely needed to submit their papers at the end of the last class. They could turn the papers in early, of course, but there was no grade benefit to doing so. I suppose they should have been happy: I had given them complete flexibility and freedom of choice. Not only that, but they also had the lowest risk of being penalized by missing an intermediate deadline.

The third class received what might be called a dictatorial treatment: I dictated three deadlines for the three papers, set at the fourth, eighth, and twelfth weeks. These were my marching orders, and they left no room for choice or flexibility.

Of these three classes, which do you think achieved the best final grades? Was it Gurev and his classmates, who had some flexibility? Or the second class, which had a single deadline at the end, and thus complete flexibility? Or the third class, which had its deadlines dictated from above, and therefore had no flexibility? Which class do you predict did worst?

When the semester was over and Jose Silva, the teaching assistant for the classes (himself an expert on procrastination and currently a professor at the University of California at Berkeley), had returned the papers to the students, we could at last compare the grades across the three different deadline conditions. We found that the students in the class with the three firm deadlines got the best grades; the class in which I set no deadlines at all (except for the final deadline), had the worst grades; and the class in which Gurev and his class-mates were allowed to choose their own three deadlines (but with penalties for failing to meet them) finished in the mid-dle, in terms of their grades for the three papers and their fi-nal grade.

What do these results suggest? First, that students do pro-crastinate (big news); and second, that tightly restricting their freedom (equally spaced deadlines, imposed from above) is the best cure for procrastination. But the biggest revelation is that simply offering the students a tool by which they could precommit to deadlines helped them achieve bet-ter grades.

What this finding implies is that the students generally understood their problem with procrastination and did some-thing to fight it when they were given the opportunity to do so, achieving relative success. But why were the grades in the self-imposed deadlines condition not as good as the grades in the dictatorial (externally imposed) deadlines condition? My feeling is this: not everyone understands their tendency to procrastinate, and even those who do recognize their ten-dency to procrastinate may not understand their problem completely. Yes, people may set deadlines for themselves, but not necessarily the deadlines that are best for getting the best performance.

When I looked at the deadlines set by the students in Gurev's class, this was indeed the case. Although the vast majority of the students in this class spaced their deadlines substantially (and got grades that were as good as those earned by students in the dictatorial condition), some did not space their deadlines much, and a few did not space their deadlines at all. The students, who did not space their deadlines sufficiently pulled the average grades of this class down. Without properly spaced deadlines—deadlines that would have forced the students to start working on their papers earlier in the semester—the final work was generally rushed and poorly written (even without the extra penalty of one percent off the grade for each day of delay).

Interestingly, these results suggest that although everyone has problems with procrastination, those who recognize and admit their weakness are in a better position to utilize the tools of precommitment to help themselves overcome it.

So THAT WAS my experience with my students. What does it have to do with everyday life? A lot, I think. Resisting temptation and instilling self-control are general human goals, and repeatedly failing to achieve them is a source of much of our misery. When I look around, I see people trying their best to do the right thing, whether they are dieters vowing to avoid a tempting dessert tray or families vowing to spend less and save more. The struggle for control is all around us. We see it in books and magazines. Radio and television airwaves are choked with messages of self-improvement and help.

And yet, for all this electronic chatter and focus in print, we find ourselves again and again in the same predicament as my students—failing over and over to reach our long-term goals. Why? Because without commitments, we keep on falling for temptation.

What's the alternative? From the experiments that I have described above, the most obvious conclusion is that when an "external voice" gives the orders, most of us will jump to attention. After all, the students for whom I set the deadlines—for whom I provided the "parental" voice—did best. Of course, barking orders, while very effective, may not always be feasible or desirable. What's a good compromise? It seems that the best course is giving people an opportunity to commit up front to their preferred path of action. This approach might not be as effective as the dictatorial treatment, but it can help push us in the right direction (perhaps even more so if we train people to do it, and give them experience in making their own deadlines).

What's the bottom line? We have problems with self-control, related to immediate and delayed gratification—no doubt there. But each of the problems we face has potential self-control mechanisms, as well. If we can't save from our paycheck, we can take advantage of our employer's automatic deduction option; if we don't have the will to exercise regularly alone, we can set a time to exercise in the company of our friends. These are the tools that we can commit to in advance, and they may help us be the kind of people we want to be.

WHAT OTHER PROCRASTINATION problems might precommitment mechanisms solve? Consider health care and consumer debt.

Health Care
Everyone knows that preventive medicine is generally more cost-effective—for both individuals and society—than our current remedial approach. Prevention means getting health

exams on a regular basis, before problems develop. But having a colonoscopy or mammogram is an ordeal. Even a cholesterol check, which requires blood to be withdrawn, is unpleasant. So while our long-term health and longevity depend on doing such tests, in the short term we procrastinate and procrastinate and procrastinate.

But can you imagine if we all got the required health exams on time? Think how many serious health problems could be caught if they were diagnosed early. Think how much cost could be cut from health-care spending, and how much misery would be saved in the process.

So how do we fix this problem? Well, we could have a dictatorial solution, in which the state (in the Orwellian sense) would dictate our regular checkups. That approach worked well with my students, who were given a deadline and performed well. In society, no doubt, we would all be healthier if the health police arrived in a van and took procrastinators to the ministry of cholesterol control for blood tests.

This may seem extreme, but think of the other dictates that society imposes on us for our own good. We may receive tickets for jaywalking, and for having our seat belts unsecured. No one thought 20 years ago that smoking would be banned in most public buildings across America, as well as in restaurants and bars, but today it is—with a hefty fine incurred by lighting up. And now we have the movement against trans fats. (Should people be deprived of heart-clogging french fries?)

Sometimes we strongly support regulations that restrain our self-destructive behaviors, and at other times we have equally strong feelings about our personal freedom. Either way, it's always a trade-off.

But if mandatory health checkups won't be accepted by

the public, what about a middle ground, like the self-imposed deadlines I gave to Gurev and his classmates (the deadlines that offered personal choice, but also had penalties attached for the procrastinators)? This might be the perfect compromise between authoritarianism, on the one hand, and what we have too often in preventive health today—complete freedom to fail.

Suppose your doctor tells you that you need to get your cholesterol checked. That means fasting the night before the blood test, driving to the lab the next morning without breakfast, sitting in a crowded reception room for what seems like hours, and finally, having the nurse come and get you so that she can stick a needle into your arm. Facing those prospects, you immediately begin to procrastinate. But suppose the doctor charged you an up-front $100 deposit for the test, refundable only if you showed up promptly at the appointed time. Would you be more likely to show up for the test?

What if the doctor asked you if you would like to pay this $100 deposit for the test? Would you accept this self-imposed challenge? Would it make you more likely to show up for the procedure? Suppose the procedure was more complicated: a colonoscopy, for instance. Would you be willing to commit to a $200 deposit, refundable only if you arrived at the appointment on time? If so, then you will have replicated the conditions that I offered Gurev's class, conditions that certainly motivated the students to be responsible for their own decisions.

How ELSE COULD we defeat procrastination in health care? Suppose we could repackage most of our medical and dental procedures so that they were predictable and easily done. Let me tell you a story that illustrates this idea.

Several years ago, Ford Motor Company struggled to find the best way to get car owners back into the dealerships for routine automobile maintenance. The problem was that the standard Ford automobile had something like 18,000 parts that might need servicing, and unfortunately they didn't all need servicing at the same time (one Ford engineer determined that a particular axle bolt needed inspection every 3,602 miles). And this was just part of the problem: since Ford had more than 20 vehicle types, plus various model years, the servicing of them all was nearly impossible to ponder. All that consumers, as well as service advisers, could do was page through volumes of thick manuals in order to determine what services were needed.

But Ford began to notice something over at the Honda dealerships. Even though the 18,000 or so parts in Honda cars had the same ideal maintenance schedules as the Ford cars, Honda had lumped them all into three "engineering intervals" (for instance, every six months or 5,000 miles, every year or 10,000 miles, and every two years or 25,000 miles). This list was displayed on the wall of the reception room in the service department. All the hundreds of service activities were boiled down to simple, mileage-based service events, which that were common across all vehicles and model years. The board had every maintenance service activity bundled, sequenced, and priced. Anyone could see when service was due, and how much it would cost.

But the bundle board was more than convenient information: It was a true procrastination-buster, as it instructed customers to get their service done at specific times and mileages. It guided them along. And it was so simple that any customer could understand it. Customers were no longer confused. They no longer procrastinated. Servicing their Hondas on time was easy.

Some people at Ford thought this was a great idea, but at first the Ford engineers fought it. They had to be convinced that, yes, drivers could go 9,000 miles without an oil change—but that 5,000 miles would align the oil change with everything else that needed to be done. They had to be convinced that a Mustang and a F-250 Super Duty truck, despite their technological differences, could be put on the same maintenance schedule. They had to be convinced that rebundling their 18,000 maintenance options into three easily scheduled service events—making maintenance as easy as ordering a Value Meal at McDonalds—was not bad engineering, but good customer service (not to mention good business). The winning argument, in fact, was that it is better to have consumers service their vehicles at somewhat compromised intervals than not to service them at all!

In the end, it happened: Ford joined Honda in bundling its services. Procrastination stopped. Ford's service bay, which had been 40 percent vacant, filled up. The dealers made money; and in just three years, Ford matched Honda's success in the service bay.

So couldn't we make comprehensive physicals and tests as simple—and, with the addition of self-imposed financial penalties (or better, a "parental" voice), bring the quality of our health way up and make the overall costs significantly less? The lesson to learn from Ford's experience is that by bundling our medical tests (and procedures) so that people remember to do them is far smarter than adhering to an erratic series of health commands that people are unwilling to follow. And so the big question: can we shape America's medical morass and make it as easy as ordering a Happy

Meal? Einstein once argued "Simplify! Simplify!" in the margins of one of his papers. And, indeed, simplification is one mark of real genius.

Savings

We could order people to stop spending, as an Orwellian edict. This would be similar to the case of my third group of students, for whom the deadline was dictated by me. But are there cleverer ways to get people to monitor their own spending? A few years ago, for instance, I heard about the "ice glass" method for reducing credit card spending. It's a home remedy for impulsive spending. You put your credit card into a glass of water and put the glass in the freezer. Then, when you impulsively decide to make a purchase, you must first wait for the ice to thaw before extracting the card. By then, your compulsion to purchase has subsided. (You can't just put the card in the microwave, of course, because then you'd destroy the magnetic strip.)

But here's another approach that is arguably better, and certainly more up-to-date. John Leland wrote a very interesting article in the *New York Times* in which he described a growing trend of self-shame: "When a woman who calls herself Tricia discovered last week that she owed $22,302 on her credit cards, she could not wait to spread the news. Tricia, 29, does not talk to her family or friends about her finances, and says she is ashamed of her personal debt. Yet from the laundry room of her home in northern Michigan, Tricia does something that would have been unthinkable—and impossible—a generation ago: She goes online and posts intimate details of her financial life, including her net worth (now a negative $38,691), the balance and finance charges on her credit cards, and the amount of debt she has paid down ($15,312) since starting the blog about her debt last year."

The article also made it clear that Tricia's blog was part of a larger trend. Apparently, there were dozens of Web sites (maybe there are thousands by now) devoted to the same kind of debt blogging (from "Poorer than You" kgazette. blogspot.com and "We're in Debt" wereindebt.com to "Make Love Not Debt makelovenotdebt.com and Tricia's Web page: bloggingawaydebt.com). Leland noted, "Consumers are asking others to help themselves develop self-control because so many companies are not showing any restraint."[7]

Blogging about overspending is important and useful, but as we saw in Chapter 5, on emotions, what we truly need is a method to curb our consumption at the moment of temptation, rather than a way to complain about it after the fact.

What could we do? Could we create something that replicated the conditions of Gurev's class, with some freedom of choice but built-in boundaries as well? I began to imagine a credit card of a different kind—a *self-control* credit card that would let people restrict their own spending behavior. The users could decide in advance how much money they wanted to spend in each category, in every store, and in every time frame. For instance, users could limit their spending on coffee to $20 every week, and their spending on clothing to $600 every six months. Cardholders could fix their limit for groceries at $200 a week and their entertainment spending at $60 a month, and not allow any spending on candy between two and five PM. What would happen if they surpassed the limit? This is what the cardholders themselves would decide. For instance, they could make the card get rejected; or they could tax themselves and transfer the tax to Habitat for Humanity, a friend, or long-term savings. This system could also implement the "ice glass" as a cooling-off period for large items; and it could even automatically trigger an e-mail to your spouse, your mother, or a friend:

> Dear Sumi,
> This e-mail it to draw your attention to the fact that your husband Dan Ariely, who is generally an upright citizen, has exceed his spending limit on chocolate of $50 per month by $73.25.
> With best wishes,
> The self-control credit card team

Now this may sound like a pipe dream, but it isn't. Think about the potential of Smart Cards (thin, palm-size cards that carry impressive computational powers), which are beginning to fill the market. These cards offer the possibility of being customized to each individual's credit needs and helping people manage their credit wisely. Why couldn't a card, for instance, have a spending "governor" (like the governors that limit the top speed on engines) to limit monetary transactions in particular conditions? Why couldn't they have the financial equivalent of a time-release pill, so that consumers could program their cards to dispense their credit to help them behave as they hope they would?

A FEW YEARS ago I was so convinced that a "control" credit card was a good idea that I asked for a meeting with one of the major banks. To my delight, this venerable bank responded, and suggested that I come to its corporate headquarters in New York.

I arrived in New York a few weeks later, and after a brief

delay at the reception desk, was led into a modern conference room. Peering through the plate glass from on high, I could look down on Manhattan's financial district, and a stream of yellow cabs pushing through the rain. Within a few minutes the room had filled with half a dozen high-powered banking executives, including the head of the bank's credit card division.

I began by describing how procrastination causes everyone problems. In the realm of personal finance, I said, it causes us to neglect our savings—while the temptation of easy credit fills our closets with goods that we really don't need. It didn't take long before I saw that I was striking a very personal chord with each of them.

Then I began to describe how Americans have fallen into a terrible dependence on credit cards, how the debt is eating them alive, and how they are struggling to find their way out of this predicament. America's seniors are one of the hardest-hit groups. In fact, from 1992 to 2004 the rate of debt of Americans age 55 and over rose faster than that of any other group. Some of them were even using credit cards to fill the gaps in their Medicare. Others were at risk of losing their homes.

I began to feel like George Bailey begging for loan forgiveness in *It's a Wonderful Life*. The executives began to speak up. Most of them had stories of relatives, spouses, and friends (not themselves, of course) who had had problems with credit debt. We talked it over.

Now the ground was ready and I started describing the self-control credit card idea as a way to help consumer spend less and save more. At first I think the bankers were a bit stunned. I was suggesting that they help consumers control their spending. Did I realize that the bankers and credit card companies made $17 billion a year in interest from these cards? Hello? They should give that up?

Well, I wasn't that naive. I explained to the bankers that there was a great business proposition behind the idea of a self-control card. "Look," I said, "the credit card business is cutthroat. You send out six billion direct-mail pieces a year, and all the card offers are about the same." Reluctantly, they agreed. "But suppose one credit card company stepped out of the pack," I continued, "and identified itself as a good guy— as an advocate for the credit-crunched consumer? Suppose one company had the guts to offer a card that would actually help consumers control their credit, and better still, divert some of their money into long-term savings?" I glanced around the room. "My bet is that thousands of consumers would cut up their other credit cards—and sign up with you!"

A wave of excitement crossed the room. The bankers nodded their heads and chatted to one another. It was revolutionary! Soon thereafter we all departed. They shook my hand warmly and assured me we would be talking again, soon.

Well, they never called me back. (It might have been that they were worried about losing the $17 billion in interest charges, or maybe it was just good old procrastination). But the idea is still there—a self-control credit card—and maybe one day someone will take the next step.

CHAPTER 7

The High Price of Ownership

Why We Overvalue What We Have

At Duke University, basketball is somewhere between a passionate hobby and a religious experience. The basketball stadium is small and old and has bad acoustics—the kind that turn the cheers of the crowd into thunder and pump everyone's adrenaline level right through the roof. The small size of the stadium creates intimacy but also means there are not enough seats to contain all the fans who want to attend the games. This by the way, is how Duke likes it; and the university has expressed little interest in exchanging the small, intimate stadium for a larger one. To ration the tickets, an intricate selection process has been developed over the years, to separate the truly devoted fans from all the rest.

Even before the start of the spring semester, students who want to attend the games pitch tents in the open grassy area outside the stadium. Each tent holds up to 10 students. The campers who arrive first take the spots closest to the stadium's entrance, and the ones who come later line up farther back. The evolving community is called Krzyzewskiville, reflecting the respect the students have for Coach K—Mike Krzyzewski—as well as their aspirations for victory in the coming season.

So that the serious basketball fans are separated from those without "Duke blue" running through their veins, an air horn is sounded at random times. At the sound, a countdown begins, and within the next five minutes at least one person from each tent must check in with the basketball authorities. If a tent fails to register within these five minutes, the whole tent gets bumped to the end of the line. This procedure continues for most of the spring semester, and intensifies in the last 48 hours before a game.

At that point, 48 hours before a game, the checks become "personal checks." At this point a tent is merely a social structure: when the air horn is sounded, every student has to check in with the basketball authorities. Missing an "occupancy check" in these final two days can mean being bumped to the end of the line. Although the air horn sounds occasionally before routine games, it can be heard at all hours of night and day before the really big contests (such as games against the University of North Carolina-Chapel Hill and during the national championships).

But that's not the oddest part of the ritual. The oddest part is that for the really important games, such as the national titles, the students at the front of the line still don't get a ticket. Rather, each of them gets a lottery number. Only later, as they crowd around a list of winners posted at the student center, do they find out if they have really, truly won a ticket to a coveted final game.

As Ziv Carmon (a professor at INSEAD, the business school based in Paris) and I listened to the air horn during the campout at Duke in the spring of 1994, we were intrigued by the real-life experiment going on before our eyes. All the students who were camping out wanted passionately to go to the basketball game. They had all camped out for a long time for the privilege. But when the lottery was over, some of them would become ticket owners, while others would not.

The question was this: would the students who had won tickets—who had ownership of tickets—value those tickets more than the students who had not won them even though they all "worked" equally hard to obtain them? Our hypothesis was that they would. We hypothesized that when we own something—whether it's a car or a violin, a cat or a basketball ticket—we begin to value it more than other people do.

Think about this for a minute. Why does the seller of a house usually value that property more than the potential buyer? Why does the seller of an automobile envision a higher price than the buyer? In many transactions why does the owner want more money than the potential owner is willing to pay? There's an old saying, "One man's ceiling is another man's floor." Well, when you're the owner, you're at the ceiling; and when you're the buyer, you're at the floor.

To be sure, that is not always the case. I have a friend who contributed a full box of record albums to a garage sale, for instance, simply because he couldn't stand hauling them around any longer. The first person who came along offered him $25 for the whole box (without even looking at the titles), and my friend accepted it. The buyer probably sold them for 10 times that price the following day. Indeed, if we always overvalued what we had, there would be no such thing as *Antique Roadshows*. ("How much did you pay for this powder horn? Five dollars? Well, let me tell you, you have a national treasure here.")

But this caveat aside, we still believed that in general the ownership of something increases its value in our eyes. Were we right? Did the students at Duke who had won the tickets—who could now anticipate experiencing the packed stands and the players racing across the court—value them more than the students who had not won them? There was only one good way to find out: an experiment.

In this case, Ziv and I would try to buy tickets from some of the students who had won them—and sell them to those who didn't. That's right; we were about to become ticket scalpers.

THAT NIGHT WE got a list of the students who had won the lottery and those who hadn't, and we started telephoning. Our first call was to William, a senior majoring in chemistry. William was rather busy. After camping for the previous week, he had a lot of homework and e-mail to catch up on. He was not too happy, either, because after reaching the front of the line, he was still not one of the lucky ones who had won a ticket in the lottery.

"Hi, William," I said, "I understand you didn't get one of the tickets for the final four."

"That's right."

"We may be able to sell you a ticket."

"Cool."

"How much would you be willing to pay for one?"

"How about a hundred dollars?" he replied.

"Too low," I laughed. "You'll have to go higher."

"A hundred fifty?" he offered.

"You have to do better" I insisted, "What's the highest price you'll pay?"

William thought for a moment. "A hundred seventy-five."

"That's it?"

"That's it. Not a penny more."

"OK, you're on the list. I'll let you know," I said. "By the way, how'd you come up with that hundred seventy-five?"

William said he figured that for $175 he could also watch the game at a sports bar, free, spend some money on beer and food, and still have a lot left over for a few CDs or even some shoes. The game would no doubt be exciting, he said, but at the same time $175 is a lot of money.

Our next call was to Joseph. After camping out for a week Joseph was also behind on his schoolwork. But he didn't care—he had won a ticket in the lottery and now, in a few days, he would be watching the Duke players fight for the national title.

"Hi, Joseph," I said, "We may have an opportunity for you—to sell your ticket. What's your minimum price."

"I don't have one."

"Everyone has a price," I replied, giving the comment my best Al Pacino tone.

His first answer was $3,000.

"Come on," I said, "That's way too much. Be reasonable; you have to offer a lower price."

"All right," he said, "twenty-four hundred."

"Are you sure?" I asked.

"That's as low as I'll go."

"OK. If I can find a buyer at that price, I'll give you a call. By the way," I added, "how did you come up with that price?"

"Duke basketball is a huge part of my life here," he said passionately. He then went on to explain that the game would be a defining memory of his time at Duke, an experience that he would pass on to his children and grandchildren. "So how can you put a price on that?" he asked. "Can you put a price on memories?"

William and Joseph were just two of over 100 students that we called. In general, the students who did not own a ticket were willing to pay around $170 for one. That price, as in William's case, was tempered by alternative uses for the money (such as spending it in a sports bar for drinks and food). Those who owned a ticket, on the other hand, demanded about $2,400 for it. Like Joseph, they talked about it in terms of the importance of the experience and the lifelong memories it would create.

What was really surprising, though, was that in all our phone calls, not a single person was willing to sell a ticket at a price that someone else was willing to pay. What did we have? We had a group of students all hungry for a basketball ticket before the lottery drawing; and then, bang—in an instant after the drawing, they were divided into two groups—ticket owners and one of non–ticket owners. It was an emotional chasm that was formed, between those who now imagined the glory of the game, and those who imagined what else they could buy with the price of the ticket. And it was an empirical chasm as well—the average selling price (about $2,400) was separated by a factor of about 14 from the average buyer's offer (about $175).

From a rational perspective, both the ticket holders and the non–ticket holders should have thought of the game in exactly the same way. After all, the anticipated atmosphere at the game and the enjoyment one could expect from the experience should not depend on winning a lottery. Then how could a random lottery drawing have changed the students' view of the game—and the value of the tickets—so dramatically?

OWNERSHIP PERVADES OUR lives and, in a strange way, shapes many of the things we do. Adam Smith wrote, "Every man [and woman] . . . lives by exchanging, or becomes in some measure a merchant, and the society itself grows to be what is properly a commercial society." That's an awesome thought. Much of our life story can be told by describing the ebb and flow of our particular possessions—what we get and what we give up. We buy clothes and food, automobiles and homes, for instance. And we sell things as well—homes and cars, and in the course of our careers, our time.

Since so much of our lives is dedicated to ownership, wouldn't it be nice to make the best decisions about this? Wouldn't it be nice, for instance, to know exactly how much we would enjoy a new home, a new car, a different sofa, and an Armani suit, so that we could make accurate decisions about owning them? Unfortunately, this is rarely the case. We are mostly fumbling around in the dark. Why? Because of three irrational quirks in our human nature.

The first quirk, as we saw in the case of the basketball tickets, is that we fall in love with what we already have. Suppose you decide to sell your old VW bus. What do you start doing? Even before you've put a for sale sign in the window, you begin to recall trips you took. You were much younger, of course; the kids hadn't sprouted into teenagers. A warm glow of remembrance washes over you and the car. This applies not only to VW buses, of course, but to everything else.

And it can happen fast.

For instance, two of my friends adopted a child from China, and told me this remarkable story. They went to China with 12 other couples. When they reached the orphanage, the director took each of the couples separately into a room and presented them with a daughter. When the couples reconvened the following morning, they all commented on the director's wisdom: Somehow she knew exactly which little girl to give to each couple. The matches were perfect, they said. My friends felt the same way, but they also realized that the matches had been random. What made each match seem perfect was not the Chinese woman's talent, but nature's ability to make us instantly attached to what we have.

The second quirk is that we focus on what we may lose, rather than what we may gain. When we price our beloved VW, therefore, we think more about what we will lose (the use of the bug) than what we will gain (money to buy something else). That's why we put it up for sale at an unrealistically high price. Likewise, the ticket holder focuses on losing the basketball experience, rather than imagining the enjoyment of obtaining money or on what can be purchased with it. Our aversion to loss is a strong emotion, and as I will explain later in the book, one that sometimes causes us to make bad decisions. Do you wonder why we refuse to sell some of our cherished clutter, and when we do sell it, attach an exorbitant price tag? Often we are already mourning the loss.

The third quirk is that we assume other people will see the transaction from the same perspective as we do. We somehow expect the buyer of our VW to share our feelings, emotions, and memories. Or we expect the buyer of our house to appreciate how the sunlight filters through the kitchen windows. Unfortunately, the buyer of the VW is more likely to notice the puff of smoke that is emitted as you shift from first into second; and the buyer of your house is more likely to notice the strip of black mold in the corner. It is just difficult for us to imagine that the person on the other side of the transaction, buyer or seller, is not seeing the world as we see it.

OWNERSHIP ALSO HAS what I'd call "peculiarities." For one, the more work you put into something, the more ownership you begin to feel for it. Think about the last time you assembled some furniture. Figuring out which piece goes where and which screw fits into which hole boosts the feeling of ownership.

In fact, I can say with a fair amount of certainty that pride of ownership is inversely proportional to the ease at which one assembles the furniture; wires the high-density television to the surround-sound system; installs software; or gets the baby into the bath, dried, powdered, diapered, and tucked away in the crib. My friend and colleague Mike Norton (a professor at Harvard) and I have a term for this phenomenon: the "Ikea effect."

Another peculiarity is that we can begin to feel ownership even before we own something. Think about the last time you entered an online auction. Suppose you make your first bid on Monday morning, for a wristwatch, and at this point you are the highest bidder. That night you log on, and you're still the top dog. Ditto for the next night. You start thinking about that elegant watch. You imagine it on your wrist; you imagine the compliments you'll get. And then you go online again one hour before the end of the auction. Some dog has topped your bid! Someone else will take your watch! So you increase your bid beyond what you had originally planned.

Is the feeling of partial ownership a cause for the upward spiral we often see in online auctions? Is it the case that the longer an auction continues, the greater grip virtual ownership will have on the various players and the more money they will spend? A few years ago, James Heyman, Yesim Orhun (a professor at the University of Chicago), and I set up an experiment to explore how the duration of an auction gradually affects the auction's participants and encourages them to bid to the bitter end. As we suspected, the participants who were the highest bidders, for the longest periods of time, ended up with the strongest feelings of virtual ownership. Of course, they were in a vulnerable position: once they thought of themselves as owners, they were compelled to prevent losing their position by bidding higher and higher.

"Virtual ownership," of course, is the mainspring of the advertising industry. We see a happy couple driving down the California coastline in a BMW convertible, and we imagine ourselves there. We get a catalog of hiking clothing from Patagonia and see a polyester fleece pullover and—poof—we start thinking of it as ours. The trap is set, and we willingly walk in. We become partial owners even before we own anything.

There's another way that we can get drawn into ownership. Often, companies will have "trial" promotions. If we have a basic cable television package, for instance, we are lured into a "digital gold package" by a special "trial" rate (only $59 a month instead of the usual $89). After all, we tell ourselves, we can always go back to basic cable or downgrade to the "silver package."

Once we try the gold package, of course, we claim ownership of it. Will we really have the strength to downgrade to basic or even to "digital silver" again? Doubtful. At the onset, we may think that we can easily return to the basic service, but once we are comfortable with the digital picture, we begin to incorporate our ownership of it into our view of the world and ourselves, and quickly rationalize away the additional price. More than that, our aversion to loss—the loss of that nice crisp "gold package" picture—is too much for us to bear. In other words, before we make the switch we may not be certain that the cost of the digital gold package is worth the full price; but once we have it, the emotions of ownership come welling up, to tell us that the loss of "digital gold" is more painful than spending a few more dollars a month. We may think we can turn back, but that is actually much harder than we expected.

Another example of the same hook is the "30-day money-back guarantee." If we are not sure whether or not we should get a new sofa, the guarantee of being able to change our mind later may push us over the hump so that we end up getting it. We might not appreciate how our perspective will shift once we have it at home, and how we will start viewing the sofa—as ours—and consequently start viewing returning it as a loss. We might think we are taking it home only to try it out for a few days, but we are unaware of the emotions the sofa can ignite in us.

OWNERSHIP IS NOT limited to material things. It can also apply to points of view. Once we take ownership of an idea—whether it's about politics or sports—what do we do? We love it perhaps more than we should. We prize it more than it is worth. And most frequently, we have trouble letting go of it—because we can't stand the idea of its loss. What are we left with then? An ideology—rigid and unyielding.

THERE IS NO known cure for the ills of ownership. As Adam Smith said, it is woven into our lives. But being aware of it might help. Everywhere around us we see the temptation to improve the quality of our lives by buying a larger home, a second car, a dishwasher, a lawn mower, and so on. But, once we change our possessions we have a very hard time going back down. As I noted earlier, ownership simply changes our perspective. Suddenly, moving backward to our pre-ownership state is a loss, one that we cannot abide. And so, while moving up in life, we indulge ourselves with the fantasy that we can always ratchet ourselves back if need be; but in reality, we can't. Downgrading to a smaller home, for instance, is experienced as a loss, it is psychologically painful, and we are willing to make all kinds of sacrifices in order to avoid such losses—even if, in this case, the monthly mortgage sinks our ship.

My own approach is to try to view each transaction (particularly a large one) as if I were a nonowner, putting some distance between myself and the item of interest. In this attempt, I'm not certain if I have achieved the uninterest in material things that is espoused by the Hindu sannyasi, but at least I try to be as Zen as I can about it.

CHAPTER 8

Keeping Doors Open

Why Options Distract Us from Our Main Objective

In 210 BC, a Chinese commander named Xiang Yu led his troops across the Yangtze River to attack the army of the Qin (Ch'in) dynasty. Pausing on the banks of the river for the night, his troops awakened in the morning to find, to their horror, that their ships were burning. They hurried to their feet to fight off their attackers, but soon discovered that it was Xiang Yu himself who had set their ships on fire, and that he had also ordered all the cooking pots crushed.

Xiang Yu explained to his troops that without the pots and the ships, they had no other choice but to fight their way to victory or perish. That did not earn Xiang Yu a place on the Chinese army's list of favorite commanders, but it did have a tremendous focusing effect on his troops: grabbing their lances and bows, they charged ferociously against the enemy and won nine consecutive battles, completely obliterating the main-force units of the Qin dynasty.

Xiang Yu's story is remarkable because it is completely

antithetical to normal human behavior. Normally, we cannot stand the idea of closing the doors on our alternatives. Had most of us been in Xiang Yu's armor, in other words, we would have sent out part of our army to tend to the ships, just in case we needed them for retreat; and we would have asked others to cook meals, just in case the army needed to stay put for a few weeks. Still others would have been instructed to pound rice out into paper scrolls, just in case we needed parchment on which to sign the terms of the surrender of the mighty Qin (which was highly unlikely in the first place).

In the context of today's world, we work just as feverishly to keep all our options open. We buy the expandable computer system, just in case we need all those high-tech bells and whistles. We buy the insurance policies that are offered with the plasma high-definition television, just in case the big screen goes blank. We keep our children in every activity we can imagine—just in case an activity may spark their interest in gymnastics, piano, French, organic gardening, or tae kwon do. And we buy a luxury SUV, not because we really expect to drive off the highway, but because just in case we do, we want to have some clearance beneath our axles.

We might not always be aware of it, but in every case we give something up for those options. We end up with a computer that has more functions than we need, or a stereo with an unnecessarily expensive warranty. And in the case of our kids, we give up their time, and ours—and the chance that they could become really good at one activity—in trying to give them some experience in all the activities. In running back and forth among the things that might be important, we forget to spend enough time on what really *is* important. It's a fool's game, and one that we are remarkably adept at playing.

I saw this precise problem in one of my undergraduate students, an extremely talented young man named Joe. As an incoming junior, Joe had just completed his required courses, and now he had to choose a major. But which one? He had a passion for architecture—he spent his weekends studying the eclectically designed buildings around Boston. He could see himself as a designer of such proud structures one day. At the same time he liked computer science, particularly the freedom and flexibility that the field offered. He could see himself with a good-paying job at an exciting company like Google. His parents wanted him to become a computer scientist—and besides, who goes to MIT to be an architect anyway? The architecture department at MIT is in fact very good. Still, his love of architecture was strong.

As Joe spoke, he wrung his hands in frustration. The classes he needed for majors in computer science and architecture were incompatible. For computer science, he needed algorithms, artificial intelligence, computer systems engineering, circuits and electronics, signals and systems, and computational structures, and a laboratory in software engineering. For architecture, he needed different courses: Experiencing Architecture Studio, Foundations in the Visual Arts, Introduction to Building Technology, Introduction to Design Computing, Introduction to the History and Theory of Architecture, and a further set of architecture studios.

How could he shut the door on one career or the other? If he started taking classes in computer science, he would have a hard time switching over to architecture; and if he started in architecture, he would have an equally difficult time switching to computer science. On the other hand, if he signed up for classes in both disciplines, he would most likely end up without a degree in either field at the end of his four years at MIT, and he would require another year (paid for by his parents) to complete his degree. (He eventually graduated with a degree in computer science, but he found the perfect blend in his first job—designing nuclear subs for the navy).

Dana, another student of mine, had a similar problem—but hers centered on two boyfriends. She could dedicate her energy and passion to a person she had met recently and, she hoped, build an enduring relationship with him. Or she could continue to put time and effort into a previous relationship that was by now dying. She clearly liked the new boyfriend better than the former one—yet she couldn't let the earlier relationship go. Meanwhile, her new boyfriend was getting restless. "Do you really want to risk losing the boy you love," I asked her, "for the remote possibility that you may discover—at some later date—that you love your former boyfriend more?" She shook her head "no," and broke into tears.*

What is it about options that is so difficult for us? Why do we feel compelled to keep as many doors open as possible, even at great expense? Why can't we simply commit ourselves?†

To try to answer these questions, Jiwoong Shin (a professor at Yale) and I devised a series of experiments that we hoped would capture the dilemma represented by Joe and Dana. In our case, the experiment would be based on a computer game that we hoped would eliminate some of the complexities of life and would give us a straightforward answer

---

*I'm often surprised by how much people confide in me. I think it's partly due to my scars, and to the obvious fact that I've been through substantial trauma. On the other hand, what I would like to believe is that people simply recognize my unique insight into the human psyche, and thus seek my advice. Either way, I have learned a lot from the stories they have shared with me.
†Matrimony is a social device that would seem to force individuals to shut down their alternative options; but, as we know, it doesn't always do so.

about whether people have a tendency to keep doors open for too long. We called it the "door game." For a location, we chose a dark, dismal place—a cavern that even Xiang Yu's army would have been reluctant to enter.

MIT's EAST CAMPUS dormitory is a daunting place. It is home to the hackers, hardware enthusiasts, oddballs, and general misfits (and believe me—it takes a serious misfit to be a misfit at MIT). One hall allows loud music, wild parties, and even public nudity. Another is a magnet for engineering students, whose models of everything from bridges to roller coasters can be found everywhere. (If you ever visit this hall, press the "emergency pizza" button, and a short time later a pizza will be delivered to you.) A third hall is painted completely black. A fourth has bathrooms adorned with murals of various kinds: press the palm tree or the samba dancer, and music piped in from the hall's music server (all downloaded legally, of course), comes on.

One afternoon a few years ago, Kim, one of my research assistants, roamed the hallways of East Campus with a laptop tucked under her arm. At each door she asked the students whether they'd like to make some money participating in a quick experiment. When the reply was in the affirmative, Kim entered the room and found (sometimes only with difficulty) an empty spot to place the laptop.

As the program booted up, three doors appeared on the computer screen: one red, the second blue, and the third green. Kim explained that the participants could enter any of the three rooms (red, blue, or green) simply by clicking on a particular door. With each subsequent click in the room they could earn a certain amount of money. If a particular room offered between one cent and 10 cents, for instance, they could make something in that range each time they clicked their mouse in that room. The screen tallied their earnings as they went along.

Getting the most money out of this experiment involved finding the room with the biggest payoff and clicking in it as many times as possible. But this wasn't trivial. Each time you moved from one room to another, you used up one click (you had a total of 100 clicks). On one hand, switching from one room to another might be a good strategy for finding the biggest payout. On the other hand, running madly from door to door (and room to room) meant that you were burning up clicks which could otherwise have made you money.

Albert, a violin player (and a resident of the Dark Lord Krotus worshippers' hall), was one of the first participants. He was a competitive type, and determined to make more money than anyone else playing the game. For his first move, he chose the red door and entered the cube-shaped room.

Once inside, he clicked the mouse. It registered 3.5 cents. He clicked again; 4.1 cents; a third click registered one cent. After he sampled a few more of the rewards in this room, his interest shifted to the green door. He clicked the mouse eagerly and went in.

Here he was rewarded with 3.7 cents for his first click; he clicked again and received 5.8 cents; he received 6.5 cents the third time. At the bottom of the screen his earnings began to grow. The green room seemed better than the red room—but what about the blue room? He clicked to go through that last unexplored door. Three clicks fell in the range of four cents. Forget it. He hurried back to the green door (the room paying about five cents a click) and spent the remainder of his 100 clicks there, increasing his payoff. At the end, Albert inquired about his score. Kim smiled as she told him it was one of the best so far.

ALBERT HAD CONFIRMED something that we suspected about human behavior: given a simple setup and a clear goal (in this case, to make money), all of us are quite adept at pursuing the source of our satisfaction. If you were to express this experiment in terms of dating, Albert had essentially sampled one date, tried another, and even had a fling with a third. But after he had tried the rest, he went back to the best—and that's where he stayed for the remainder of the game.

But to be frank, Albert had it pretty easy. Even while he was running around with other "dates," the previous ones waited patiently for him to return to their arms. But suppose that the other dates, after a period of neglect, began to turn their backs on him? Suppose that his options began to close down? Would Albert let them go? Or would he try to hang on to all his options for as long as possible? In fact, would he sacrifice some of his guaranteed payoffs for the privilege of keeping these other options alive?

To find out, we changed the game. This time, any door left unvisited for 12 clicks would disappear forever.

SAM, A RESIDENT of the hackers' hall, was our first participant in the "disappearing" condition. He chose the blue door to begin with; and after entering it, he clicked three times. His earnings began building at the bottom of the screen, but this wasn't the only activity that caught his eye. With each additional click, the other doors diminished by one-twelfth, signifying that if not attended to, they would vanish. Eight more clicks and they would disappear forever.

Sam wasn't about to let that happen. Swinging his cursor around, he clicked on the red door, brought it up to its full size, and clicked three times inside the red room. But now he noticed the green door—it was four clicks from disappearing. Once again, he moved his cursor, this time restoring the green door to its full size.

The green door appeared to be delivering the highest payout. So should he stay there? (Remember that each room had a range of payouts. So Sam could not be completely convinced that the green door was actually the best. The blue might have been better, or perhaps the red, or maybe neither.) With a frenzied look in his eye, Sam swung his cursor across the screen. He clicked the red door and watched the blue door continue to shrink. After a few clicks in the red, he jumped over to the blue. But by now the green was beginning to get dangerously small—and so he was back there next.

Before long, Sam was racing from one option to another, his body leaning tensely into the game. In my mind I pictured a typically harried parent, rushing kids from one activity to the next.

Is this an efficient way to live our lives—especially when another door or two is added every week? I can't tell you the answer in terms of your personal life, but in our experiments we saw clearly that running from pillar to post was not only stressful but uneconomical. In fact, in their frenzy to keep doors from shutting, our participants ended up making substantially less money (about 15 percent less) than the students who didn't have to deal with closing doors. The truth is that they could have made more money by picking a room—any room—and merely staying there for the whole experiment!

(Think about that in terms of your life or career.)

When Jiwoong and I tilted the experiments against keeping options open, the results were still the same. For instance, we made each door-click cost three cents, so that the cost was not just the loss of a click (an opportunity cost) but also a direct financial loss. There was no difference in response from our participants. They still had the same irrational excitement about keeping their options open.

Then we told the participants the exact monetary outcomes they could expect from each room. The results were still the same. They still could not stand to see a door close. Also, we allowed some participants to experience hundreds of practice trials before the actual experiment. Certainly, we thought, they would see the wisdom of *not* pursuing the closing doors. But we were wrong. Once they saw their options shrinking, our MIT students—supposedly among the best and brightest of young people—could not stay focused. Pecking like barnyard hens at every door, they sought to make more money, and ended up making far less.

In the end, we tried another sort of experiment, one that smacked of reincarnation. In this condition, a door would still disappear if it was not visited within 12 clicks. But it wasn't gone forever. Rather, a single click could bring it back to life. In other words, you could neglect a door without any loss. Would this keep our participants from clicking on it anyhow? No. To our surprise, they continued to waste their clicks on the "reincarnating" door, even though its disappearance meant nothing and could be easily reversed. They just couldn't tolerate the idea of the loss, and so they did whatever was necessary to prevent their doors from closing.

How can we unshackle ourselves from this irrational impulse to chase worthless options? In 1941 the philosopher Erich Fromm wrote a book called *Escape from Freedom*. In a modern democracy, he said, people are beset not by a lack of opportunity, but by a dizzying abundance of it. In our modern society this is emphatically so. We are continually reminded that we can do anything and be anything we want to be. The problem is in living up to this dream. We must develop ourselves in every way possible; must taste every aspect of life; must make sure that of the 1,000 things to see before dying, we have not stopped at number 999. But then comes a problem—are we spreading ourselves too thin? The temptation Fromm was describing, I believe, is what we saw as we watched our participants racing from one door to another.

Running from door to door is a strange enough human activity. But even stranger is our compulsion to chase after doors of little worth—opportunities that are nearly dead, or that should be of little interest to us any longer. My student Dana, for instance, had already concluded that one of her suitors was most likely a lost cause. Then why did she jeopardize her relationship with the other man by continuing to nourish the wilting relationship with the less appealing romantic partner? Similarly, how many times have we bought something on sale not because we really needed it but because by the end of the sale all of those items would be gone, and we could never have it at that price again?

The other side of this tragedy develops when we fail to realize that some things really are disappearing doors, and need our immediate attention. We may work more hours at our jobs, for instance, without realizing that the childhood of our sons and daughters is slipping away. Sometimes these doors close too slowly for us to see them vanishing. One of my friends told me, for instance, that the single best year of his marriage was when he was living in New York, his wife was living in Boston, and they met only on weekends. Before they had this arrangement—when they lived together in Boston—they would spend their weekends catching up on work rather than enjoying each other. But once the arrangement changed, and they knew that they had only the weekends together, their shared time became limited and had a clear end (the time of the return train). Since it was clear that the clock was ticking, they spent more time enjoying each other than doing their work.

I'm not advocating giving up work for your children's sake or moving to a different city just to improve your weekends with your spouse (although it might provide some benefits). But wouldn't it be nice to have a built-in alarm, to warn us when the doors are closing on our most important options?

So what can we do? In our experiments, we proved that running helter-skelter to keep doors from closing is a fool's game. It will not only wear out our emotions but also wear out our wallets. What we need is to consciously start closing some of our doors. Small doors, of course, are rather easy to close. We can easily strike names off our holiday card lists, for instance, or omit the tae kwon do from our daughter's string of activities.

But the bigger doors (or those that seem bigger) are harder to close. Doors that just might lead to a new career or to a better job might be hard to close. Doors that are tied to our dreams are also hard to close. So are relationships with certain people—even if they seem to be going nowhere.

We have an irrational compulsion to keep doors open. It's just the way we're wired. But that doesn't mean we shouldn't try to close them. Think about a fictional episode: Rhett Butler leaving Scarlett O'Hara, in the scene when she clings to him in and begs him, "Where shall I go? What shall I do?" Rhett, after enduring too much from Scarlett, and finally having his fill of it, says, "Frankly, my dear, I don't give a damn." It's not by chance that this line in the film version of Margaret Mitchell's novel has been voted the most memorable in cinematographic history. It's the emphatic closing of a door that gives it widespread appeal. And it should be a reminder to all of us that we have doors—little and big ones—which we ought to shut.

We need to drop out of committees that are a waste of our time, and stop sending holiday cards to people who have moved on to other lives and friends. We need to determine whether we really have time to watch basketball and play both golf and squash and keep our family together; perhaps we should put these sports behind us. We ought to shut them because they draw energy and commitment away from the doors that should be left open—and because they drive us crazy.

SUPPOSE YOU'VE CLOSED so many of your doors that you have just two left. I wish I could say that your choices are easier now, but often they are not. In fact, choosing between two things that are similarly attractive is one of the most difficult decisions we can make. This is a situation not just of keeping options open for too long, but of being indecisive to the point of paying for our indecision in the end. Let me use the following story to explain.

A hungry donkey approaches a barn one day looking for hay and discovers two haystacks of identical size at the two opposite sides of the barn. The donkey stands in the middle of the barn between the two haystacks, not knowing which to select. Hours go by, but he still can't make up his mind. Eventually the donkey dies of starvation.

This story is hypothetical, of course, and casts unfair aspersions on the intelligence of donkeys. A better example might be the U.S. Congress. Congress frequently gridlocks itself, not necessarily with regard to the big picture of particular legislation—the restoration of the nation's aging highways, immigration improving federal protection of endangered species, etc.—but with regard to the details. Often, to a reasonable person, the party lines on these issues are the equivalent of the two bales of hay. Despite this, or because of it, Congress is frequently left stuck in the middle. Wouldn't a quick decision have been better for everybody?

Here's another example. One of my friends spent three months selecting a digital camera from two nearly identical models. When he finally made his selection, I asked him how many photo opportunities had he missed, how much of his valuable time he had spent making the selection, and how much he would have paid to have digital pictures of his family and friends documenting the last three months. More than the price of the camera, he said. Has something similar happened to you?

What my friend (and also the donkey and Congress) failed to do when focusing on the minor similarities and differences between two things was to take into account the *consequences of not deciding*. The donkey failed to consider starving, Congress failed to consider the lives lost while it debated highway legislation, and my friend failed to consider all the great pictures he was missing, not to mention the time he was spending at Best Buy. More important, they all failed to take into consideration the relatively minor differences that would have come with either one of the decisions.

My friend would have been equally happy with either camera; the donkey could have eaten either bale of hay; and the members of Congress could have gone home crowing over their accomplishments, regardless of the slight difference in bills. In other words, they all should have considered the decision an easy one. They could have even flipped a coin (figuratively, in the case of the donkey) and gotten on with their lives. But we don't act that way, because we just can't close those doors.

ALTHOUGH CHOOSING BETWEEN two very similar options should be simple, in fact it is not. I fell victim to this very same problem a few years ago, when I was considering whether to stay at MIT or move to Stanford (I chose MIT in the end). I spent several weeks comparing the two schools closely, and found that, overall, they were about the same in their overall attractiveness to me. So what did I do? At this stage of my problem, I decided I needed some more information and research on the ground. So I visited both schools. I met people at each place and asked them how they liked it. I checked out neighborhoods and possible schools for our kids. Sumi and I pondered how the two options would fit in with the kind of life we wanted for ourselves. Before long, I was getting so engrossed in this decision that my academic research and productivity began to suffer. Ironically, as I searched for the best place to do my work, my research was being neglected.

Since you have probably invested some money to purchase my wisdom in this book (not to mention time, and the other activities you have given up in the process), I should probably not readily admit that I wound up like the donkey, trying to discriminate between two very similar bales of hay. But I did.

In the end, and with all my foreknowledge of the difficulty in this decision-making process, I was just as predictably irrational as everyone else.

CHAPTER 9

The Effect of Expectations

Why the Mind Gets What It Expects

Suppose you're a fan of the Philadelphia Eagles and you're watching a football game with a friend who, sadly, grew up in New York City and is a rabid fan of the Giants. You don't really understand why you ever became friends, but after spending a semester in the same dorm room you start liking him, even though you think he's football-challenged.

The Eagles have possession and are down by five points with no time-outs left. It's the fourth quarter, and six seconds are left on the clock. The ball is on the 12-yard line. Four wide receivers line up for the final play. The quarterback hikes the ball and drops back in the pocket. As the receivers sprint toward the end zone, the quarterback throws a high pass just as the time runs out. An Eagles wide receiver near the corner of the end zone dives for the ball and makes a spectacular catch.

The referee signals a touchdown and all the Eagles players run onto the field in celebration. But wait. Did the receiver get both of his feet in? It looks close on the Jumbotron; so the booth calls down for a review. You turn to your friend: "Look at that! What a great catch! He was totally in. Why are they even reviewing it?" Your friend scowls. "That was completely out! I can't believe the ref didn't see it! You must be crazy to think that was in!"

What just happened? Was your Giants-fan friend the Giants fan just experiencing wishful thinking? Was he deceiving himself? Worse, was he lying? Or had his loyalty to his team—and his anticipation of its win—completely, truly, and deeply clouded his judgment?

I was thinking about that one evening, as I strolled through Cambridge and over to MIT's Walker Memorial building. How could two friends—two honest guys—see one soaring pass in two different ways? In fact, how could any two parties look at precisely the same event and interpret it as supporting their opposing points of view? How could Democrats and Republicans look at a single schoolchild who is unable to read, and take such bitterly different positions on the same issue? How could a couple embroiled in a fight see the causes of their argument so differently?

A friend of mine who had spent time in Belfast, Ireland, as a foreign correspondent, once described a meeting he had arranged with members of the IRA. During the interview, news came that the governor of the Maze prison, a winding row of cell blocks that held many IRA operatives, had been assassinated. The IRA members standing around my friend, quite understandably, received the news with satisfaction—as a victory for their cause. The British, of course, didn't see it in those terms at all. The headlines in London the next day boiled with anger and calls for retribution. I am an Israeli, and no stranger to such cycles of violence. Violence is not rare. It happens so frequently that we rarely stop to ask ourselves why. Why does it happen? Is it an outcome of history, or race, or politics—or is there something fundamentally irrational in us that encourages conflict, that causes us to look at the same event and, depending on our point of view, see it in totally different terms?

Leonard Lee (a professor at Columbia), Shane Frederick (a professor at MIT), and I didn't have any answers to these profound questions. But in a search for the root of this human condition, we decided to set up a series of simple experiments to explore how previously held impressions can cloud our point of view. We came up with a simple test—one in which we would not use religion, politics, or even sports as the indicator. We would use glasses of beer.

YOU REACH THE entrance to Walker by climbing a set of broad steps between towering Greek columns. Once inside (and after turning right), you enter two rooms with carpeting that predates the advent of electric light, furniture to match, and a smell that has the unmistaken promise of alcohol, packs of peanuts, and good company. Welcome to the Muddy Charles—one of MIT's two pubs, and the location for a set of studies that Leonard, Shane, and I would be conducting over the following weeks. The purpose of our experiments would be to determine whether people's expectations influence their views of subsequent events—more specifically, whether bar patrons' expectations for a certain kind of beer would shape their perception of its taste.

Let me explain this further. One of the beers that would be served to the patrons of the Muddy Charles would be

Budweiser. The second would be what we fondly called MIT Brew. What's MIT Brew? Basically Budweiser, plus a "secret ingredient"—two drops of balsamic vinegar for each ounce of beer. (Some of the MIT students objected to our calling Budweiser "beer"; so in subsequent studies, we used Sam Adams—a substance more readily acknowledged by Bostonians as "beer.")

At about seven that evening, Jeffrey, a second-year PhD student in computer science, was lucky enough to drop by the Muddy Charles. "Can I offer you two small, free samples of beer?" asked Leonard, approaching him. When Jeffrey agreed, Leonard led him over to a table that held two pitchers of the foamy stuff, one labeled A and the other B. Jeffrey sampled a mouthful of one of them, swishing it around thoughtfully, and then sampled the other. "Which one would you like a large glass of?" asked Leonard. Jeffrey thought it over. With a free glass in the offing, he wanted to be sure he would be spending his near future with the right malty friend.

Jeffrey chose beer B as the clear winner, and joined his friends (who were in deep conversation over the cannon that a group of MIT students had recently "borrowed" from the Caltech campus). Unbeknownst to Jeffrey, the two beers he had previewed were Budweiser and the MIT Brew—and the one he selected was the vinegar-laced MIT brew.

A few minutes later, Nina, a visiting student from Germany, dropped in. "Like a free beer?" asked Leonard. Her reply was a smile and a nod of the head. This time, Leonard offered more information. Beer A, he explained, was a standard commercial beer, whereas beer B had been doctored with a few drops of balsamic vinegar. Nina tasted the two beers. After finishing the samples (and wrinkling her nose at the vinegar-laced brew B) she gave the nod to beer A. Leonard poured her a large glass of the commercial brew and Nina happily joined her friends at the pub.

Nina and Jeffrey were only two of hundreds of students who participated in this experiment. But their reaction was typical: without foreknowledge about the vinegar, most of them chose the vinegary MIT Brew. But when they knew in advance that the MIT brew had been laced with balsamic vinegar, their reaction was completely different. At the first taste of the adulterated suds, they wrinkled their noses and requested the Budweiser instead. The moral, as you might expect, is that if you tell people up front that something might be distasteful, the odds are good that they will end up agreeing with you—not because their experience tells them so but because of their expectations.

If, at this point in the book, you are considering the establishment of a new brewing company, especially one that specializes in adding some balsamic vinegar to beer, consider the following points: (1) If people read the label, or knew about the ingredient, they would most likely hate your beer. (2) Balsamic vinegar is actually pretty expensive—so even if it makes beer taste better, it may not be worth the investment. Just brew a better beer instead.

BEER WAS JUST the start of our experiments. The MBA students at MIT's Sloan school also drink a lot of coffee. So one week, Elie Ofek (a professor at the Harvard Business School), Marco Bertini (a professor at the London Business School), and I opened an impromptu coffee shop, at which we offered students a free coffee if they would answer a few questions about our brew. A line quickly formed. We handed our participants their cups of coffee and then pointed them to a table set with coffee additives—milk, cream, half-and-half, white sugar, and brown sugar. We also set out some unusual condiments—cloves, nutmeg, orange peel, anise, sweet paprika, and cardamom—for our coffee drinkers to add to their cups.

After adding what they wanted (and none of our odd condiments was ever used) and tasting the coffee, the participants filled out a survey form. They indicated how much they liked the coffee, whether they would like it served in the cafeteria in the future, and the maximum price they would be willing to pay for this particular brew.

We kept handing out coffee for the next few days, but from time to time we changed the containers in which the odd condiments were displayed. Sometimes we placed them in beautiful glass-and-metal containers, set on brushed metal tray with small silver spoons and nicely printed labels. At other times we placed the same odd condiments in white Styrofoam cups. The labels were handwritten in a red felt-tip pen. We went further and not only cut the Styrofoam cups shorter, but gave them jagged, hand-cut edges.

What were the results? No, the fancy containers didn't persuade any of the coffee drinkers to add the odd condiments (I guess we won't be seeing sweet paprika in coffee anytime soon). But the interesting thing was that when the odd condiments were offered in the fancy containers, the coffee drinkers were much more likely to tell us that they liked the coffee a lot, that they would be willing to pay well for it, and that they would recommend that we should start serving this new blend in the cafeteria. When the coffee ambience looked upscale, in other words, the coffee tasted upscale as well.

WHEN WE BELIEVE beforehand that something will be good, therefore, it generally will be good (and when we think it will be bad, it will bad). But how deep are these influences? Do they just change our beliefs, or do they also change the physiology of the experience itself? In other words, can previous knowledge actually modify the neural activity underlying the taste itself, so that when we expect something to taste good (or bad), it will actually taste that way?

To test this possibility, Leonard, Shane, and I conducted the beer experiments again, but with an important twist. We had already tested our MIT Brew in two ways—by telling our participants about the presence of vinegar in the beer *before* they tasted the brew, and by not telling them anything at all about it. But suppose we initially didn't tell them about the vinegar, then had them taste the beer, then revealed the presence of the vinegar, and then asked for their reactions. Would the placement of the knowledge—coming just after the experience—evoke a different response from what we received when the participants got the knowledge before the experience?

For a moment, let's switch from beer to another example. Suppose you heard that a particular sports car was fantastically exciting to drive, took one for a test drive, and then gave your impressions of the car. Would your impressions be different from those of people who didn't know anything about the sports car, took the test drive, then heard the car was hot, and then wrote down their impressions? In other words, does it matter if knowledge comes before or after the experience? And if so, which type of input is the more important—knowledge before the experience, or an input of information after an experience has taken place?

The significance of this question is that if knowledge

merely informs us of a state of affairs, then it shouldn't matter whether our participants received the information before or after tasting the beer: in other words, if we told them up front that there was vinegar in the beer, this should affect their review of the beer. And if we told them afterward, that should similarly affect their review. After all, they both got the same bad news about the vinegar-laced beer. This is what we should expect if knowledge merely *informs* us.

On the other hand, if telling our participants about the vinegar at the outset actually reshapes their sensory perceptions to align with this knowledge, then the participants who know about the vinegar up front should have a markedly different opinion of the beer from those who swigged a glass of it, and then were told. Think of it this way. If knowledge actually modifies the taste, then the participants who consumed the beer before they got the news about the vinegar, tasted the beer in the same way as those in the "blind" condition (who knew nothing about the vinegar). They learned about the vinegar only after their taste was established, at which point it was too late for the knowledge to affect the sensory perceptions.

So did the students who were told about the vinegar after tasting the beer like it as little as the students who learned about the vinegar before tasting the beer? Or did they like it as much as the students who never learned about the vinegar? What do you think?

As it turned out, the students who found out about the vinegar after drinking the beer liked the beer better than those who were told about the vinegar up front. In fact, those who were told afterward about the vinegar liked the beer just as much as those who weren't aware that there was any vinegar in the beer at all.

What does this suggest? Let me give you another example. Suppose Aunt Darcy is having a garage sale, trying to get rid of many things she collected during her long life. A car pulls up, some people get out, and before long they are gathered around one of the oil paintings propped up against the wall. Yes, you agree with them, it does look like a fine example of early American primitivism. But do you tell them that Aunt Darcy copied it from a photograph just a few years earlier?

My inclination, since I am an honest, upright person, would be to tell them. But should you tell them before or after they finish admiring the painting? According to our beer studies, you and Aunt Darcy would be better off keeping the information under wraps until after the examination. I'm not saying that this would entice the visitors to pay thousands for the painting (even though our beer drinkers preferred our vinegar-laced beer as much when they were told after drinking it as when they were not told at all), but it might certainly get you a higher price for Aunt Darcy's work.

By the way, we also tried a more extreme version of this experiment. We told one of two groups in advance about the vinegar (the "before" condition) and told the second group about the vinegar after they had finished the sampling (the "after" condition). Once the tasting was done, rather than offer them a large glass of their choice, we instead gave them a large cup of unadulterated beer, some vinegar, a dropper, and the recipe for the MIT Brew (two drops of balsamic vinegar per ounce of beer). We wanted to see if people would freely add balsamic vinegar to their beer; if so, how much they would use; and how these outcomes would depend on whether the participants tasted the beer before or after knowing about the vinegar.

What happened? Telling the participants about the vinegar after rather than before they tasted the beer doubled the number of participants who decided to add vinegar to their beer. For the participants in the "after" condition, the beer with vinegar didn't taste too bad the first time around (they apparently reasoned), and so they wouldn't mind giving it another try.*

As you see, expectations can influence nearly every aspect of our life. Imagine that you need to hire a caterer for your daughter's wedding. Josephine's Catering boasts about its "delicious Asian-style ginger chicken" and its "flavorful Greek salad with kalamata olives and feta cheese." Another caterer, Culinary Sensations, offers a "succulent organic breast of chicken roasted to perfection and drizzled with a merlot demi-glace, resting in a bed of herbed Israeli cous-cous" and a "mélange of the freshest roma cherry tomatoes and crisp field greens, paired with a warm circle of chèvre in a fruity raspberry vinagrette."

Although there is no way to know whether Culinary Sensations' food is any better than Josephine's, the sheer depth of the description may lead us to expect greater things from the simple tomato and goat cheese salad. This, accordingly, increases the chance that we (and our guests, if we give them the description of the dish) will rave over it.

This principle, so useful to caterers, is available to everyone. We can add small things that sound exotic and fashionable to our cooking (chipotle-mango sauces seem all the rage right now; or try buffalo instead of beef). These ingredients

---

*As noted, we were also hoping to measure the amount of vinegar students added to the beer. But everyone who added vinegar added the amount specified in the recipe.

might not make the dish any better in a blind taste test; but by changing our expectations, they can effectively influence the taste when we have this pre-knowledge.

These techniques are especially useful when you are inviting people for dinner—or persuading children to try new dishes. By the same token, it might help the taste of the meal if you omit the fact that a certain cake is made from a commercial mix or that you used generic rather than brand-name orange juice in a cocktail, or, especially for children, that Jell-O comes from cow hooves. (I am not endorsing the morality of such actions, just pointing to the expected outcomes.)

Finally, don't underestimate the power of presentation. There's a reason that learning to present food artfully on the plate is as important in culinary school as learning to grill and fry. Even when you buy take-out, try removing the Styrofoam packaging and placing the food on some nice dishes and garnishing it (especially if you have company); this can make all the difference.

These suggestions are particularly close to my heart, because, in addition to my career as a behavioral economist, I am the aspiring author of a (yet to be published) cooking guide (tentatively titled, "Dining without Crumbs: The Art of Eating over the Sink"). One more piece of advice: If you want to enhance the experience of your guests, invest in a nice set of wineglasses.

Moreover, if you're really serious about your wine, you may want to go all out and purchase the glasses that are specific to burgundies, chardonnays, champagne, etc. Each type of glass is supposed to provide the appropriate environment, which should bring out the best in these wines (even though controlled studies find that the shape of the glass makes no difference at all in an objective blind taste, that doesn't stop people from perceiving a significant difference when they are handed the "correct glass"). Moreover, if you forget that the shape of the glass really has no effect on the taste of the wine, you yourself may be able to better enjoy the wine you consume in the correct fancy glasses.

Expectations, of course, are not limited to food. When you invite people to a movie, you can increase their enjoyment by mentioning that it got great reviews. This is also essential for building the reputation of a brand or product. That's what marketing is all about—providing information that will heighten someone's anticipated and real pleasure. But do expectations created by marketing really change our enjoyment?

I'm sure you remember the famous "Pepsi Challenge" ads on television (or at least you may have heard of them). The ads consisted of people chosen at random, tasting Coke and Pepsi and remarking about which they liked better. These ads, created by Pepsi, announced that people preferred Pepsi to Coke. At the same time, the ads for Coke proclaimed that people preferred Coke to Pepsi. How could that be? Were the two companies fudging their statistics?

The answer is in the different ways the two companies evaluated their products. Coke's market research was said to be based on consumers' preferences when they could see what they were drinking, including the famous red trademark. While Pepsi ran its challenge using blind tasting and standard plastic cups marked M and Q. Could it be that Pepsi tasted better in a blind taste test but that Coke tasted better in a non-blind (sighted) test?

To better understand the puzzle of Coke versus Pepsi, a terrific group of neuroscientists—Sam McClure, Jian Li, Damon Tomlin, Kim Cypert, Latané Montague, and Read Montague—conducted their own blind and non-blind taste test of Coke and Pepsi. The modern twist on this test was supplied by a functional magnetic resonance imaging (fMRI) machine. With the machine, the researchers could monitor the activity of the participants' brains while they consumed the drinks.

Tasting drinks while one is in an fMRI is not simple, by the way, because a person whose brain is being scanned must lie perfectly still. To overcome this problem, Sam and his colleagues put a long plastic tube into the mouth of each participant, and from a distance injected the appropriate drink (Pepsi or Coke) through the tube into their mouths. As the participants received a drink, they were also presented with visual information indicating either that that Coke was coming, that Pepsi was coming, or that some drink was coming. This way the researchers could observe the brain activation of the participants while they consumed Coke and Pepsi, both when they knew which beverage they were drinking and when they did not.

What were the results? In line with the Coke and Pepsi "challenges," it turned out that the brain activation of the participants was different depending on whether the name of the drink was revealed or not. This is what happened. Whenever a person received a squirt of Coke or Pepsi, the center of the brain associated with strong feelings of emotional connection—called the ventromedial prefrontal cortex, VMPFC—was stimulated. But when the participants knew they were going to get a squirt of Coke, something additional happened. This time, the frontal area of the brain—the dorsolateral aspect of the prefrontal cortex, DLPFC, an area involved in higher human brain functions like working memory, associations, and higher-order cognitions and ideas—was also activated. To be sure it happened with Pepsi—but even more so with Coke (and, naturally, the response was stronger in people who had a stronger preference for Coke).

The reaction of the brain to the basic hedonic value of the drinks (essentially sugar) turned out to be similar for the two drinks. But the advantage of Coke over Pepsi was due to Cokes's brand—which activated the higher-order brain mechanisms. These associations, then, and not the chemical properties of the drink, gave Coke its advantage in the marketplace.

It is also interesting to consider the ways in which the frontal part of the brain is connected to the pleasure center. There is a dopamine link by which the front part of the brain projects and activates the pleasure centers. This is probably why Coke was liked more when the brand was known—the associations were more powerful, allowing the part of the brain that represents these associations to enhance activity in the brain's pleasure center. This should be good news to any ad agency, of course, because it means that the bright red can, swirling script, and the myriad messages that have come down to consumers over the years (such as "Things go better with . . .") are as much responsible for our love of Coke as the brown bubbly stuff inside.

EXPECTATIONS ALSO SHAPE stereotypes. A stereotype, after all, is a way of categorizing information, in the hope of predicting experiences. The brain cannot start from scratch at every new situation. It must build on what it has seen before. For that reason, stereotypes are not intrinsically malevolent. They provide shortcuts in our never-ending attempt to make sense of complicated surroundings. This is why we have the expectation that an elderly person will need help using a computer or that a student at Harvard will be intelligent.* But because a stereotype provides us with specific expectations about members of a group, it can also unfavorably influence both our perceptions and our behavior.

Research on stereotypes shows not only that we react differently when we have a stereotype of a certain group of people, but also that stereotyped people themselves react differently when they are aware of the label that they are forced to wear (in psychological parlance, they are "primed" with this label). One stereotype of Asian-Americans, for instance, is that they are especially gifted in mathematics and science. A common stereotype of females is that they are weak in mathematics. This means that Asian-American women could be influenced by both notions.

In fact, they are. In a remarkable experiment, Margaret Shin, Todd Pittinsky, and Nalini Ambady asked Asian-American women to take an objective math exam. But first they divided the women into two groups. The women in one group were asked questions related to their gender. They were asked about their opinions and preferences regarding coed dorms, thereby priming their thoughts for gender-related issues. The women in the second group were asked questions related to their race. These questions referred to the languages they knew, the languages they spoke at home, and their family's history in the United States, thereby priming the women's thoughts for race-related issues.

The performance of the two groups differed in a way that

---

*There is a nice T-shirt on sale at the MIT bookstore that reads "Harvard: Because not everyone can get into MIT."

matched the stereotypes of both women and Asian-Americans. Those who had been reminded that they were women performed worse than those who had been reminded that they were Asian-American. These results show that even our own behavior can be influenced by our stereotypes, and that activation of stereotypes can depend on our current state of mind and how we view ourselves at the moment.

Perhaps even more astoundingly, stereotypes can also affect the behavior of people who are not even part of a stereotyped group. In one notable study, John Bargh, Mark Chen, and Lara Burrows had participants complete a scrambled-sentence task, rearranging the order of words to form sentences (we discussed this type of task in Chapter 4). For some of the participants, the task was based on words such as *aggressive*, *rude*, *annoying*, and *intrude*. For others, the task was based on words such as *honor*, *considerate*, *polite*, and *sensitive*. The goal of these two lists was to prime the participants to think about politeness or rudeness as a result of constructing sentences from these words (this is a very common technique in social psychology, and it works amazingly well).

After the participants completed the scrambled-sentence task, they went to another laboratory to participate in what was purportedly a second task. When they arrived at the second laboratory, they found the experimenter apparently in the midst of trying to explain the task to an uncomprehending participant who was just not getting it (this supposed participant was in fact not a real participant but a confederate of the experimenter). How long do you think it took the real participants to interrupt the conversation and ask what they should do next?

The amount of waiting depended on what type of words

had been involved in the scrambled-sentence task. Those who had worked with the set of polite words patiently waited for about 9.3 minutes before they interrupted, whereas those who had worked with the set of rude words waited only about 5.5 minutes before interrupting.

A second experiment tested the same general idea by priming the concept of the elderly, using words such as *Florida*, *bingo*, and *ancient*. After the participants in this experiment completed the scrambled-sentence task, they left the room, thinking that they had finished the experiment—but in fact the crux of the study was just beginning. What truly interested the researchers was how long it would take the participants to walk down the hallway as they left the building. Sure enough, the participants in the experimental group were affected by the "elderly" words: their walking speed was considerably slower than that of a control group who had not been primed. And remember, the primed participants were not themselves elderly people being reminded of their frailty—they were undergraduate students at NYU.

WHAT ALL THE experiments teach us is that expectations are more than the mere anticipation of a boost from a fizzy Coke. Expectations enable us to make sense of a conversation in a noisy room, despite the loss of a word here and there, and likewise, to be able to read text messages on our cell phones, despite the fact that some of the words are scrambled. And although expectations can make us look foolish from time to time, they are also very powerful and useful.

So what about our football fans and the game-winning pass? Both were watching the same game—but through markedly different lenses. One saw the pass as in bounds.

The other saw it as foul. In sports, such arguments are not particularly damaging—in fact, they can be fun. The problem is that these same biased processes can influence how we experience other aspects of our world. These biased processes are, in fact a major source of escalation in almost every conflict, whether Israeli-Palestinian, American-Iraqi, Serbian-Croatian, or Indian-Pakistani.

In all these conflicts, individuals from both sides can read similar history books and even have the same facts taught to them, yet it is very unusual to find individuals who would agree about who started the conflict, who is to blame, who should make the next concession, etc. In such matters, our investment in our beliefs is much stronger than any affiliation to sport teams, and so we hold onto these beliefs tenaciously. Thus the likelihood of agreement about "the facts" becomes smaller and smaller as personal investment in the problem grows. This is clearly disturbing. We like to think that sitting at the same table together will help us hammer out our differences and that concessions will soon follow. But history has shown us that this is an unlikely outcome; and now we know the reason for this catastrophic failure.

But there's reason for hope. In our experiments, tasting beer without knowing about the vinegar, or learning about the vinegar after the beer was tasted, allowed the true flavor to come out. The same approach should be used to settle arguments: The perspective of each side is presented without the affiliation—the facts are revealed, but not which party took which actions. This type of "blind" condition might help us better recognize the truth.

When stripping away our preconceptions and our previous knowledge is not possible, perhaps we can at least acknowledge that we are all biased. With that recognition, we may be able to accept the idea that conflicts generally require a neutral third party to set down the rules and regulations. We are trapped within our perspective, which partially blinds us to the truth, and we need a neutral third party who has not been tainted with our expectations. Of course, accepting the word of a third party is not easy and not always possible; but when it is possible, it can yield substantial benefits. And for that reason alone, we must continue to try.

CHAPTER 10

The Power of Price

*Why a 50-Cent Aspirin Can Do What
a Penny Aspirin Can't*

If you were living in 1950 and had chest pain, your cardiologist might well have suggested a procedure for angina pectoris called internal mammary artery ligation. In this operation, the patient is anesthetized, the chest is opened at the sternum, and the internal mammary artery is tied off. Voilà! Pressure to the pericardiophrenic arteries is raised, blood flow to the myocardium is improved, and everyone goes home happy.[8]

So this was an apparently successful operation, and it had been a popular one for the previous 20 years. But one day in 1955 cardiologist in Seattle, Leonard Cobb, and a few colleagues became suspicious. Was it really an effective procedure? Did it really work? Cobb decided to try to prove the efficacy of the procedure in a very bold way: he would perform the operation on half his patients, and fake the procedure on the other half. Then he would see which group felt better, and whose health actually improved. In other words, after 25 years of filleting patients like fish, heart surgeons would finally get a scientifically controlled surgical trial to see how effective the procedure really was.

To carry out this test, as noted above, Dr Cobb performed the traditional procedure on some of the patients, and placebo surgery on the others. The real surgery, again as noted above, meant opening the patient up and tying up the internal mammary artery. In the placebo procedure, the surgeon merely cut into the patient's flesh with a scalpel, leaving two incisions. Nothing else was done.

The results were startling. Both the patients who did have their mammary veins constricted and those who didn't reported immediate relief from their chest pain. In both groups, the relief lasted about three months—and then complaints about chest pain returned. Meanwhile, electrocardiograms showed no difference between those who had undergone the real operation and those who got the placebo operation. In other words, the traditional procedure seemed to provide some short-time relief—but so did the placebo. In the end, neither procedure provided significant long-term relief.

More recently a different medical procedure was submitted to a similar test, with surprisingly similar results. As early as 1993, J. B. Moseley, an orthopedic surgeon, had increasing doubts about the use of arthroscopic surgery for a particular arthritic affliction of the knee. Did the procedure really work? Recruiting 180 patients with osteoarthritis from the veterans' hospital in Houston, Dr. Moseley and his colleagues divided them into three groups.

One group got the standard treatment: anesthetic, three incisions, scopes inserted, cartilage removed, correction of soft-tissue problems, and 10 liters of saline washed through the knee. The second group got anesthesia, three incisions, scopes inserted, and 10 liters of saline, but no cartilage was removed. The third group—the placebo group—looked from the outside like the other two treatments anesthesia, incisions, etc.; and the procedure took the same amount of time; but no instruments were inserted into the knee. In other words, this was simulated surgery.[9]

For two years following the surgeries, all three groups (which consisted of volunteers, as in any other placebo experiment) were tested for a lessening of their pain, and for the amount of time it took them to walk and climb stairs. How did they do? The groups that had the full surgery and the arthroscopic lavage were delighted, and said they would recommend the surgery to their families and friends. But strangely—and here was the bombshell—the placebo group also got relief from pain and improvements in walking—to the same extent, in fact, as those who had the actual operations. Reacting to this startling conclusion, Dr. Nelda Wray, one of the authors of the Moseley study, noted, "The fact that the effectiveness of arthroscopic lavage and debridement in patients with osteoarthritis of the knee is no greater than that of placebo surgery makes us question whether the $1 billion spent on these procedures might be put to better use."

If you assume that a firestorm must have followed this report, you're right. When the study appeared on July 11, 2002, as the lead article the *New England Journal of Medicine*, some doctors screamed foul and questioned the method and results of the study. In response, Dr. Moseley argued that his study had been carefully designed and carried out. "Surgeons . . . who routinely perform arthroscopy are undoubtedly embarrassed at the prospect that the placebo effect—not surgical skill—is responsible for patient improvement after the surgeries they perform. As you might imagine, these surgeons are going to great lengths to try to discredit our study."

Regardless of the extent to which you believe the results of this study, it is clear that we should be more suspicions about arthroscopic surgery for this particular condition, and at the same time increase the burden of proof for medical procedures more generally.

In Chapter 9 we saw that expectations change the way we perceive and appreciate experiences. Exploring the placebo effect in this chapter, we'll see not only that beliefs and expectations affect how we perceive and interpret sights, tastes, and other sensory phenomena, but also that our expectations can affect us by altering our subjective and even objective experiences—sometimes profoundly so.

Most important, I want to probe an aspect of placebos that is not yet fully understood. It is the role that *price* plays in this phenomenon. Does a pricey medicine make us feel better than a cheap medicine? Can it actually make us *physiologically* better than a cheaper brand? What about expensive procedures, and new generation apparatuses, such as digital pacemakers and high-tech stents? Does their price influence their efficacy? And if so, does this mean that the bill for health care in America will continue to soar? Well, let's start at the beginning.

Placebo comes from the Latin for "I shall please." The term was used in the fourteenth century to refer to sham mourners who were hired to wail and sob for the deceased at funerals. By 1785 it appeared in the *New Medical Diction-*

ary, attached to marginal practices of medicine.

One of the earliest recorded examples of the placebo effect in medical literature dates from 1794. An Italian physician named Gerbi made an odd discovery: when he rubbed the secretions of a certain type of worm on an aching tooth, the pain went away for a year. Gerbi went on to treat hundreds of patients with the worm secretion, keeping meticulous records of their reactions. Of his patients, 68 percent reported that their pain, too, went away for a year. We don't know the full story of Gerbi and his worm secretions, but we have a pretty good idea that the secretions really had nothing to do with curing toothaches. The point is that Gerbi believed they helped—and so did a majority of his patients.

Of course, Gerbi's worm secretion wasn't the only placebo in the market. Before recent times, almost all medicines were placebos. Eye of the toad, wing of the bat, dried fox lungs, mercury, mineral water, cocaine, an electric current: these were all touted as suitable cures for various ailments. When Lincoln lay dying across the street from Ford's Theater, it is said that his physician applied a bit of "mummy paint" to the wounds. Egyptian mummy, ground to a powder, was believed to be a remedy for epilepsy, abscesses, rashes, fractures, paralysis, migraine, ulcers, and many other things. As late as 1908, "genuine Egyptian mummy" could be ordered through the E. Merck catalog—and it's probably still in use somewhere today.[10]

Mummy powder wasn't the most macabre of medicines, though. One seventeenth-century recipe for a "cure all" medication advised: "Take the fresh corpse of a red-haired, uninjured, unblemished man, 24 years old and killed no more than one day before, preferably by hanging, breaking on the wheel or impaling. . . . Leave it one day and one night in the light of the sun and the moon, then cut into shreds or rough strips. Sprinkle on a little powder of myrrh and aloes, to prevent it from being too bitter."

We may think we're different now. But we're not. Placebos still work their spell over us. For years, surgeons cut remnants of scar tissue out of the abdomen, for instance, imagining that this procedure addressed chronic abdominal pain—until researchers faked the procedure in controlled studies and patients reported equal relief.[11] Encainide, flecainide, and mexiletine were widely prescribed off-label drugs for irregular heartbeat—and were later found to cause cardiac arrest.[12] When researchers tested the effect of the six leading antidepressants, they noted that 75 percent of the effect was duplicated in placebo controls.[13] The same was true of brain surgery for Parkinson's disease.[14] When physicians drilled holes in the skulls of several patients without performing the full procedure, to test its efficacy, the patients who received the sham surgery had the same outcome as those who received the full procedure. And of course the list goes on and on.

One could defend these modern procedures and compounds by noting that they were developed with the best intentions. This is true. But so were the applications of Egyptian mummy, to a great extent. And sometimes, the mummy powder worked just as well as (or at least no worse than) whatever else was used.

The truth is that placebos run on the power of suggestion. They are effective because people believe in them. You see your doctor and you feel better. You pop a pill and you feel better. And if your doctor is a highly acclaimed specialist, or your prescription is a new wonder drug of some kind, you feel even better. But how does suggestion influence us?

IN GENERAL, TWO mechanisms shape the expectations that make placebos work. One is belief—our confidence or faith in the drug, the procedure, or the caregiver. Sometimes just the fact that a doctor or nurse is paying attention to us and reassuring us not only makes us feel better but also triggers our internal healing processes. Even a doctor's enthusiasm for a particular treatment or procedure may predispose us toward a positive outcome.

The second mechanism is conditioning. Like Pavlov's famous dogs (that learned to salivate at the ring of a bell), the body builds up expectancy after repeated experiences. Suppose you've ordered pizza. When the deliveryman presses the doorbell, your digestive juices start flowing even before you can smell the pie. Or suppose that you are on your honeymoon and you've snuggled up on the couch with your loved one. As you're sitting there staring into a crackling fire, the prospect of sex releases endorphins, preparing you for what is to come next, and sending your sense of well-being into the stratosphere.

In the case of pain, expectation can unleash hormones and neurotransmitters, such as endorphins and opiates, that not only block agony but produce exuberant highs (endorphins trigger the same receptors as cocaine). I vividly recall lying in the burn ward in terrible pain, for instance. As soon as I saw the nurse approaching, with a needle almost dripping with painkiller, what relief! My brain began secreting pain-dulling opioids, even before the needle broke my skin.

Thus familiarity may or may not breed contempt, but it definitely breeds expectations. Branding, packaging, and the reassurance of the caregiver can make us feel better. But what about price? Can the price of a drug also affect our response to it?

ON THE BASIS of price alone, it is easy to imagine that a $4,000 couch will be more comfortable than a $400 couch; that a pair of designer jeans will be better stitched and more comfortable than a pair from Wal-Mart; that a high-grade electric sander will work better than a low-grade sander; and that the roast duck at the Imperial Dynasty (for $19.95) is substantially better than the roast duck at Wong's Noodle Shop (for $10.95); But can such implied difference in quality influence the actual experience, and can such influence also apply to objective experiences such as our reactions to pharmaceuticals?

For instance, would a cheaper painkiller be less effective than a more expensive one? Would your winter cold feel worse if you took a discount cold medicine than if you took an expensive one? Would your asthma respond less well to a generic drug than to the latest brand-name on the market? In other words, are drugs like Chinese food, sofas, blue jeans, and tools? Can we assume that high price means higher quality, and do our expectations translate into the objective efficacy of the product?

This is a particularly important question. The fact is that you can get away with cheaper Chinese food and less expensive jeans. With some self-control, we can usually steer ourselves away from the most expensive brands. But will you really look for bargains when it comes to your health? Putting the common cold aside for the moment; are many of us going to pinch pennies when our lives are at risk? No—we want the best, for ourselves, our children and our loved ones.

If we want the best for ourselves, does an expensive drug makes us feel better than a cheaper drug? Does cost really make a difference in how we feel? In a series of experiments a few years ago, that's what Rebecca Waber (a graduate student at MIT), Baba Shiv (a professor at Stanford), Ziv Carmon, and I decided to find out.

IMAGINE THAT YOU'RE taking part in an experiment to test the efficacy of a new painkiller called Veladone-Rx. (The actual experiment involved about 100 adult Bostonians, but for now, we'll let you take their place.)

You arrive at the MIT media lab in the morning. Taya Leary, a young woman wearing a crisp business suit (this is in stark contrast to the usual attire of the students and faculty at MIT) greets you warmly, with a hint of a Russian accent. A photo ID identifies Taya as a representative of Vel Pharmaceuticals. She invites you to spend a moment reading a brochure about Veladone-Rx. Glancing around, you note that the room looks like a medical office: stale copies of *Time* and *Newsweek* are scattered around; brochures for Veladone-Rx are spread out on the table; and nearby is a cup of pens, with the drug's handsome logo. "Veladone is an exciting new medication in the opioid family," you read. "Clinical studies show that over 92 percent of patients receiving Veladone in double-blind controlled studies reported significant pain relief within only 10 minutes, and that pain relief lasted up to eight hours." And how much does it cost? According to the brochure, $2.50 for a single dose.

Once you finish reading the brochure, Taya calls in Rebecca Waber and leaves the room. Rebecca, wearing the white coat of a lab technician, with a stethoscope hanging from her neck, asks you a set of questions about your medical condition and your family's medical history. She listens to your heart and measures your blood pressure. Then she hooks you up to a complicated-looking machine. The electrodes running from the machine, greased with a green electrode gel, encircle your wrists. This is an electrical shock generator, she explains, and it is how we will test your perception and tolerance of pain?

With her hand on the switch, Rebecca sends a series of electrical shocks through the wires and into the electrodes. The initial shocks are merely annoying. Then they become painful, more painful, and finally so painful that your eyes fly open and your heart begins to race. She records your reactions. Now she starts delivering a new set of electrical shocks. This time she administers a set of charges that fluctuate randomly in intensity: some are very painful and some merely irritating. Following each one, you are asked to record, using the computer in front of you, the amount of pain you felt. You use the mouse to click on a line that ranges from "not painful at all" to "extremely painful" (this is called a "visual pain analog").

When this part of the torture ends, you look up. Rebecca is standing before you with a Veladone capsule in one hand and a cup of water in the other. "It will take about 15 minutes for the drug to reach its maximal effect," she says. You gulp it down, and then move to a chair in the corner, where you look at the old copies of *Time* and *Newsweek* until the pill takes effect.

Fifteen minutes later Rebecca, smearing the electrodes with the same green electrode gel, cheerfully asks, "Ready for the next step?" You say nervously, "As ready as I can be." You're hooked up to the machine again, and the shocks begin. As before, you record the intensity of the pain after each shock. But this time it's different. It must be the Veladone-Rx! The pain doesn't feel nearly as bad. You leave with a pretty high opinion of Veladone. In fact, you hope to see it in the neighborhood drugstore before long.

Indeed, that's what most of our participants found. Almost all of them reported less pain when they experienced the electrical shocks under the influence of Veladone. Very interesting—considering that Veladone was just a capsule of vitamin C.

FROM THIS EXPERIMENT, we saw that our capsule did have a placebo effect. But suppose we priced the Veladone differently. Suppose we discounted the price of a capsule of Veladone-Rx from $2.50 to just 10 cents. Would our participants react differently?

In our next test, we changed the brochure, scratching out the original price ($2.50 per pill) and inserting a new discount price of 10 cents. Did this change our participants' reaction? Indeed. At $2.50 almost all our participants experienced pain relief from the pill. But when the price was dropped to 10 cents, only half of them did.

Moreover, it turns out that this relationship between price and placebo effect was not the same for all participants, and the effect was particularly pronounced for people who had more experience with recent pain. In other words, for people who had experienced more pain, and thus depended more on pain medications, the relationship was more pronounced: they got less benefit when the price was discounted. When it comes to medicines, then, we learned that you get what you pay for. Price can change the experience.

INCIDENTALLY, WE GOT corroborating results in another test,

a study we conducted one miserably cold winter at the University of Iowa. In this case we asked a group of students to keep track of whether they used full-price or discount medicines for their seasonal colds, and if so, how well those remedies worked. At the end of the semester, 13 participants said they'd paid list price and 16 had bought discount drugs. Which group felt better? I think you can guess by now: the 13 who paid the list price reported significantly better medical outcomes than the 16 who bought the medication at a discount. And so, in over-the-counter cold medication, what you pay is often what you get.

From our experiments with our "pharmaceuticals" we saw how prices drive the placebo effect. But do prices affect everyday consumer products as well? We found the perfect subject in SoBe Adrenaline Rush, a beverage that promises to "elevate your game" and impart "superior functionality."

In our first experiment, we stationed ourselves at the entrance of the university's gym, offering the SoBe. The first group of students paid the regular price for the drink. A second group also purchased the drink, but for them the price was marked down to about half the regular price. After the students exercised, we asked them if they felt more or less fatigued relative to how they normally felt after their usual workouts. Both groups of students who drank the SoBe indicated that they were somewhat less fatigued than usual. That seemed plausible, especially considering the hefty shot of caffeine in each bottle of SoBe.

But it was the effect of the price, not the effect of the caffeine, that we were after. Would higher-priced SoBe reduce fatigue better than the half-price SoBe? As you can imagine from the experiment with Veladone, it did. The students who drank the higher-priced beverage reported less fatigue than those who had the half-price drink.

That experiment was interesting, but it was based on the participants' impressions of their own state—their subjective reports. How could we test SoBe more directly and objectively? We found a way: SoBe claims to provide "energy for your mind." So we decided to test that claim by using a series of word puzzles.

It would work like this. Half of the students would buy their SoBe at full price, and the other half would buy it at a discount. (We actually charged their student accounts, so in fact their parents were being billed.) After consuming the drinks, the students would be asked to watch a movie for 10 minutes (to allow the effects of the beverage to sink in, we explained). Then we would give each of them a 15-word puzzle, with 30 minutes to solve as many of the problems as they could. (For example, when given the set TUPPIL, participants had to rearrange it to PULPIT—or they would have to rearrange FRIVEY and SVALIE to get . . .):

Word puzzles

Lunike	_____
epsoop	_____
quinue	_____
lefziz	_____
frivey	_____
quiety	_____
nyglik	_____
yennit	_____
rancor	_____
tuppil	_____

bewolb	_____
raclan	_____
rethie	_____
svalie	_____
berkam	_____

We had already established a baseline, having given the word-puzzle test to a group of students who had not drunk SoBe. This group got on average nine of the 15 items right. What happened when we gave the puzzles to the students who drank SoBe? The students who had bought it at the full price also got on average about nine answers right—this was no different from the outcome for those who had no drink at all. But more interesting were the answers from the half-price group: they averaged 6.5 questions right. What can we gather from this? Price does make a difference, and in this case the difference was a gap of about 28 percent in performance on the word puzzles.

So SoBe didn't make anyone smarter. Does this mean that the product itself is a dud (at least in terms of solving word puzzles)? To answer this question, we devised another test. The following message was printed on the cover of the quiz booklet: "Drinks such as SoBe have been shown to improve mental functioning," we noted, "resulting in improved performance on tasks such as solving puzzles." We also added some fictional information, stating that SoBe's Web site referred to more than 50 scientific studies supporting its claims.

What happened? The group that had the full-price drinks still performed better than those that had the half-price drinks. But the message on the quiz booklet also exerted some influence. Both the half-price group and the full-price group, having absorbed the information and having been primed to expect success, did better than the groups whose quiz cover didn't have the message. And this time the SoBe did make people smarter. When we hyped the drink by stating that 50 scientific studies found SoBe to improve mental functioning, those who got the drink at the discount price solved on average 0.6 additional question, but those who got both the hype and the full price solved on average 3.3 additional questions. In other words, the message on the bottle (and the quiz cover) as well as the price was arguably more powerful than the beverage inside.

ARE WE DOOMED, then, to get lower benefits every time we get a discount? If we rely on our irrational instincts, we will. If we see a half-price item, we will instinctively assume that its quality is less than that of a full-price item—and then in fact we will make it so. What's the remedy? If we stop and rationally consider the product versus the price, we can break free of the unconscious urge to discount quality along with price.

We tried this in a series of experiments, and found that consumers who stop to reflect about the relationship between price and quality are far less likely to assume that a half-price drink is less effective (and, consequently, they don't perform as poorly on word puzzles as the would if they did assume it). These results not only suggest a way to overcome the relationship between price and the placebo effect but also suggest that the effect of discounts is largely an unconscious reaction to lower prices.

SO WE'VE SEEN how pricing drives the efficacy of placebo,

painkillers, and energy drinks. But here's another thought. If placebos can make us feel better, should we simply sit back and enjoy them? Or are placebos patently bad—shams that should be discarded, whether they make us feel good or not? Before you answer this question, let me raise the ante. Suppose you found a placebo substance or a placebo procedure that not only made you feel better but actually made you physically better. Would you still use it? What if you were a physician? Would you prescribe medications that were only placebos? Let me tell you a story that helps explain what I'm suggesting.

In AD 800, Pope Leo III crowned Charlemagne emperor of the Romans, thus establishing a direct link between church and state. From then on the Holy Roman emperors, followed by the kings of Europe, were imbued with the glow of divinity. Out of this came what was called the "royal touch"—the practice of healing people. Throughout the Middle Ages, as one historian after another chronicled, the great kings would regularly pass through the crowds, dispensing the royal touch. Charles II of England (1630–1685), for instance, was said to have touched some 100,000 people during his reign; and the records even include the names of several American colonists, who returned to the Old World from the New World just to cross paths with King Charles and be healed.

Did the royal touch really work? If no one had ever gotten better after receiving the royal touch, the practice would obviously have withered away. But throughout history, the royal touch was said to have cured thousands of people. Scrofula, a disfiguring and socially isolating disease often mistaken for leprosy, was believed to be dispelled by the royal touch. Shakespeare wrote in *Macbeth*, Act IV, scene 3: "Strangely visited people, All sworn and ulcerous, pitiful to the eye . . . Put on with holy prayers and 'tis spoken, the healing benediction." The royal touch continued until the 1820s, by which time monarchs were no longer considered heaven-sent—and (we might imagine) "new, improved!" advances in Egyptian mummy ointments made the royal touch obsolete.

When people think about a placebo such as the royal touch, they usually dismiss it as "just psychology." But, there is nothing "just" about the power of a placebo, and in reality it represents the amazing way our mind controls our body. How the mind achieves these amazing outcomes is not very clear. Some of the effect, to be sure, has to do with reducing the level of stress, changing hormonal secretions, changing the immune system, etc. The more we understand the connection between brain and body, the more things that once seemed clear-cut become ambiguous. Nowhere is this as apparent as with the placebo.

In reality, physicians provide placebos all the time. For instance, a study done in 2003 found that more than one-third of patients who received antibiotics for a sore throat were later found to have viral infections, for which an antibiotic does absolutely no good (and possibly contributes to the rising number of drug-resistant bacterial infections that threaten us all[15]). But do you think doctors will stop handing us antibiotics when we have viral colds? Even when doctors know that a cold is viral rather than bacterial (and many colds are viral), they still seem to feel that the patient wants some sort of relief; most commonly, the patients expect to walk out with a prescription. Is it right for the physician to fill this psychic need?

The fact that physicians give placebos all the time does not mean that they want to do this, and I suspect that the practice tends to make them somewhat uncomfortable.

They've been trained to see themselves as men and women of science, people who must look to the highest technologies of modern medicine for answers. They want to think of themselves as real healers, not practitioners of voodoo. So it can be extremely difficult for them to admit, even to themselves, that their job may include promoting health through the placebo effect. Now suppose that a doctor does allow, however grudgingly, that a treatment he knows to be a placebo helps some patients. Should he enthusiastically prescribe it? After all, the physician's enthusiasm for a treatment can play a real role in its efficacy.

Here's another question, about our national commitment to health care. America already spends more of its GDP per person on health care than any other western nation. How do we deal with the fact that expensive medicine (the 50-cent aspirin) may make people feel better than cheaper medicine (the penny aspirin). Do we indulge people's irrationality, thereby raising the costs of health care? Or do we insist that people get the cheapest generic drugs (and medical procedures) on the market, regardless of the increased efficacy of the more expensive drugs? How do we structure the cost and co-payment of treatments to get the most out of medications, and how can we provide discounted drugs to needy populations without getting them a treatment that is less effective? These are central and complex issues for structuring our health care system.

Placebos pose dilemmas for marketers, too. Their profession requires them to create perceived value. Hyping a product beyond what can be objectively proved is—depending on the degree of hype—stretching the truth or outright lying. But we've seen that the perception of value, in medicine, soft drinks, drugstore cosmetics, or cars, can become real value. If people actually get more satisfaction out of a product, has the marketer done anything worse than sell the sizzle along with the steak? As we start thinking more about placebos and the blurry boundary between beliefs and reality, these questions become more difficult to answer.

As a scientist I value experiments that test our beliefs and the efficacy of different treatments. At the same time, it is also clear to me that experiments, particularly those involving medical placebos, raise many important ethical questions. Indeed, the experiment involving mammary ligation that I mentioned at the beginning of this chapter raised an ethical issue: there was an outcry against performing sham operations on patients.

The idea of sacrificing the well-being and perhaps even the life of some individuals in order to learn whether a particular procedure should be used on other people at some point in the future is indeed difficult to swallow. Visualizing a child getting a placebo treatment for cancer just so that years later other people will perhaps get better treatment seems a strange and difficult trade-off to make.

At the same time, the trade-offs we make by *not* carrying on placebo experiments are also hard to accept. And as we have seen they can result in hundreds or thousands of people undergoing useless (but risky) operations. In the United States very few surgical procedures are tested scientifically. For that reason, we don't really know whether many operations really effect a cure, or whether, like many of their predecessors, they are merely effective because of their placebo effect. Thus, we may find ourselves frequently submitting to procedures and operations that if more carefully studied, would be put aside. Let me share with you my own story of a procedure that, in my case, was highly touted, but in reality was nothing more than a painful experience for me.

I had been in the hospital for two long months when my occupational therapist came to me with exciting news. There was a technological garment for people like me called the Jobst suit. It was skinlike, and it would add pressure to what little skin I had left, so that my skin would heal better. She told me that it was made at a factory in Ireland, and at one in America. I would get such a suit, tailored exactly to my size. She told me I would need to wear trousers, a shirt, gloves, and a mask on my face and that, since they fit exactly, they would press against my skin all the time, and when I moved, the Jobst suit would slightly massage my skin, causing the redness and the hypergrowth of the scars to decrease.

How excited I was! Shula, the physiotherapist, would tell me about how wonderful the Jobst was. She told me that it was made in different colors, and immediately I imagined myself covered from head to toe in a tight blue skin, like Spiderman; but Shula cautioned me that the colors were only brown for white people and black for black people. She told me that people used to call the police when a person wearing the Jobst mask went into a bank, because they thought it was a bank robber. Now when you get the mask from the factory, there is a sign you have to put on your chest, explaining the situation.

Rather than deterring me, this new information made the suit seem even better. It made me smile. I thought it would be nice to walk in the streets and actually be invisible. No one would be able to see any part of me except my mouth and my eyes. And no one would be able to see my scars.

As I imagined this silky cover, I felt I could endure any pain until my Jobst suit arrived. Weeks went by. And then it did arrive. Shula came to help me put it on for the first time.

We started with the trousers: She opened them, in all their brownish glory, and started to put them on my legs. The feeling wasn't silky like something that would gently massage my scars. The material felt more like canvas that would tear my scars. I was still by no means disillusioned. I wanted to feel how it would be to be immersed completely in the suit.

After a few minutes it became apparent that I had gained some weight since the time when the measurements were taken (they used to feed me 7,000 calories and 30 eggs a day to help my body heal). The Jobst suit didn't fit very well. Still, I had waited a long time for it. Finally, with some stretching and a lot of patience on everyone's part, I was eventually completely dressed. The shirt with the long sleeves put great pressure on my chest, shoulders, and arms. The mask pressed hard all the time. The long trousers began at my toes and went al the way up to my belly button. And there were the gloves. The only visible parts of me were the ends of my toes, my eyes, my ears, and my mouth. Everything else was covered by the brown Jobst.

The pressure seemed to become stronger every minute. The heat inside was intense. My scars had a poor blood supply, and the heat made the blood rush to them and made them red and much more itchy. Even the sign warning people that I was not a bank robber was a failure. The sign was in English, not Hebrew, and so was quite worthless. My lovely dream had failed me. I struggled out of the suit. New measurements were taken and sent to Ireland so that I could get a better-fitting Jobst.

The next suit provided a more comfortable fit, but otherwise it was not much better. I suffered with this treatment for months—itching, aching, struggling to wear it, and tearing my delicate new skin while trying to put it on (and when this new thin skin tears, it takes a long while to heal). At the end I learned that this suit had no real benefits, at least not for me. The areas of my body that were better covered looked and felt no different from the areas that were not as well covered, and the suffering that went along with the suit turned out to be all that it provided me.

You see, while it would be morally questionable to make patients in the burn department take part in an experiment that was designed to test the efficacy of this suit (using different types of fabrics, different pressure levels, etc.), and even more difficult to ask someone to participate in a placebo experiment, it is also morally difficult to inflict painful treatments on many patients and for many years, without having a really good reason to do so.

If this type of synthetic suit had been tested relative to other methods, and relative to a placebo suit, that approach might have eliminated part of my daily misery. It might also have stimulated research on new approaches—ones that would actually work. My wasted suffering, and the suffering of other patients like me, is the real cost of not doing such experiments.

Should we always test every procedure and carry out placebo experiments? The moral dilemmas involved in medical and placebo experiments are real. The potential benefits of such experiments should be weighed against their costs, and as a consequence we cannot, and should not, always do placebo tests. But my feeling is that we are not doing nearly as many of them as we should.

CHAPTER 11

The Context of Our Character, Part I

*Why We Are Dishonest, and What
We Can Do about It*

In 2004, the total cost of all robberies in the United States was $525 million, and the average loss from a single robbery was about $1,300, which means that the average take-home pay for such crimes is relatively low.[16] This total cost is not high, considering the amount of police, judicial, and corrections muscle put into their capture and confinement of robbers—let alone the amount of newspaper and television coverage that these kinds of crimes elicit. I'm not suggesting we go easy on career criminals, of course. They are thieves, and we must protect ourselves from their acts.

But consider this: every year, employees' theft and fraud at the workplace is estimated at about $600 billion. That's much more than the combined financial cost of robbery, burglary, larceny-theft, and automobile theft (about $16 billion in 2004); it is more than what millions of career criminals steal in their lifetimes; and it's also almost twice the market capitalization of General Electric. But there's much more. Each year, according to reports by the insurance industry, individuals add a bogus $24 billion to their claims of property losses. The IRS, meanwhile, estimates a loss of $350 billion per year, representing the gap between what the feds think people should pay in taxes and what they do pay. The retail industry has its own headache: it loses $16 billion a year to customers who buy clothes, wear them with the tags tucked in, and return these secondhand clothes for a full refund.

Add to this sundry everyday examples of dishonesty—the congressman accepting golfing junkets from his favorite lobbyist; the physician making kickback deals with the laboratories that he uses; the corporate executive who backdates his stock options to boost his final pay—and you have a huge amount of unsavory economic activity, dramatically larger than that of the average household crooks.

When the Enron scandal erupted in 2001 (and it became apparent that Enron, as *Fortune* magazine's "America's Most Innovative Company" for six consecutive years, owed much of its success to innovations in accounting), Nina Mazar (a professor at the University of Toronto), On Amir (a professor at the University of California at San Diego), and I found ourselves discussing the subject of honesty over lunch. Why are some crimes, particularly white-collar crimes, variety, judged less severely than others, we wondered—especially since their perpetrators can inflict more financial damage between the ten o'clock latte and lunch than a standard-issue burglar might in a lifetime?

After some discussion we decided that there might be two types of dishonesty. One is the type of dishonesty that evokes the image of a pair of crooks circling a gas station. As they cruise by, they consider how much money is in the till, who might be around to stop them, and what punishment they may face if caught (including how much time off they might get for good behavior). On the basis of this cost-benefit calculation, they decide whether to rob the place or not.

Then there is the second type of dishonesty. This is the kind committed by people who generally consider themselves honest—the men and women (please stand) who have "borrowed" a pen from a conference site, taken an extra splash of soda from the soft drink dispenser, exaggerated the cost of their television on their property loss report, or falsely reported a meal with Aunt Nava as a business expense (well, she did inquire about how work was going).

We know that this second kind of dishonesty exists, but how prevalent is it? Furthermore, if we put a group of "honest" people into a scientifically controlled experiment and tempted them to cheat, would they? Would they compromise their integrity? Just how much would they steal? We decided to find out.

THE HARVARD BUSINESS School holds a place of distinction in American life. Set on the banks of the River Charles in Cambridge Massachusetts, housed in imposing colonial-style architecture, and dripping with endowment money, the school is famous for creating America's top business leaders. In the Fortune 500 companies, in fact, about 20 percent of the top three positions (in each of the 500) are held by graduates of the Harvard Business School.* What better place,

---

*As claimed by the Harvard Business School.

then, to do a little experiment on the issue of honesty?*

The study would be fairly simple. We would ask a group of Harvard undergraduates and MBA students to take a test consisting of 50 multiple-choice questions. The questions would be similar to those on standardized tests (What is the longest river in the world? Who wrote *Moby Dick*? What word describes the average of a series? Who, in Greek mythology, was the goddess of love?) The students would have 15 minutes to answer the questions. At the end of that time, they would be asked to transfer their answers from their worksheet to a scoring sheet (called a bubble sheet), and submit both the worksheet, and the bubble sheet to a proctor at the front of the room. For every correct answer, the proctor would hand them 10 cents. Simple enough.

In another setup we asked a new group of students to take the same general test, but with one important change. The students in this section would take the test and transfer their work to their scoring bubble sheet, as the previous group did. But this time the bubble sheet would have the correct answers pre marked. For each question, one of the bubbles, the one indicating the correct answer, was colored gray. If the students indicated on their worksheet that the longest river in the world is the Mississippi, for instance, they would clearly see from the pre-marked bubble sheet that the right answer is the Nile.

After they transferred their answers, they counted how many questions they had answered correctly, wrote that number at the top of their bubble sheet, and handed both the worksheet and the bubble sheet to the proctor at the front of

---

* We often conduct our experiments at Harvard, not because we think its students are different from MIT's students, but because it has wonderful facilities and the faculty members are very generous in letting us use them.

the room. The proctor looked at the number of questions they claimed to have answered correctly (the summary number they wrote at the top of the bubble sheet) and paid them 10 cents per correct answer.

Would the students cheat—changing their wrong answers to the ones pre-marked on the bubble sheet? We weren't sure, but in any case, we decided to tempt the next group of students even more. In this condition the students would again take the test and transfer their answers to the pre-marked bubble sheet. But this time we would instruct them to shred their original worksheet, and hand only the bubble sheet to the proctor. In other words, they would destroy all evidence of any possible malfeasance. Would they take the bait? Again, we didn't know.

In the final condition, we would push the group's integrity to the limit. This time they would be instructed to destroy not only their original worksheet, but the final pre-marked bubble sheet as well. Moreover, they wouldn't even have to report their earnings to the experimenter: When they were finished shredding their answer sheets, they merely needed to walk up to the front of the room—where we had placed a jar full of coins—withdraw their earnings, and saunter out the door. If one was ever inclined to cheat, this was the opportunity to pull off the perfect crime.

Yes, we were tempting them. We were making it easy to cheat. Would the crème de la crème of America's youth take the bait? We'd have to see.

As the first group settled into their seats, we explained the rules and handed out the tests. They worked for their 15 minutes, then copied their answers onto the bubble sheet, and turned in their worksheets and bubble sheets. These students were our control group. Since they hadn't been given any of the answers, they had no opportunity at all to cheat. On average, they got 32.6 out the 50 questions right.

What do you predict that the participants in our experiments did? Given that the participants in the control condition solved on average 32.6 questions correctly, how many questions do you think the participants in the other three conditions claimed to have solved correctly?

Condition 1	Control	= <u>32.6</u> .
Condition 2	Self-check	= _____ .
Condition 3	Self-check + shredding	= _____ .
Condition 4	Self-check + shredding +money jar	= _____ .

What about the second group? They too answered the questions. But this time, when they transferred their answers to the bubble sheet, they could see the correct answers. Would they sweep their integrity under the rug for an extra 10 cents per question? As it turned out, this group solved on average 36.2 questions. Were they smarter than our control group? Doubtful. Instead, we had caught them in a bit of cheating.

What about the third group? This time we upped the ante. They not only got to see the correct answers but were also asked to shred their worksheets. Did they take the bait? Yes, they cheated. On average they solved 35.9 questions correctly—more than the participants in the control condition, but about the same as the participants in the second group (the group that did not shred their worksheets).

Finally came the students who were told to shred not only their worksheets but the bubble sheets as well—and then dip their hands into the money jar and withdraw whatever they wanted. Like angels they shredded their worksheets, stuck their hands into the money jar, and withdrew their coins. The problem was, these angels had dirty faces: their claims added up to an average 36.1 correct answers—quite a bit higher than the 32.6 of our control group, but basically the same as the other two groups who had the opportunity to cheat.

What did we learn from this experiment? The first conclusion, is that when given the opportunity, many honest people will cheat. In fact, rather than finding that a few bad apples weighted the averages, we discovered that the majority of people cheated, and that they cheated just a little bit.* And before you blame the refined air at the Harvard Business School for this level of dishonesty, I should add that we conducted similar experiments at MIT, Princeton, UCLA, and Yale with similar results.

The second, and more counterintuitive, results were even more impressive: Once tempted to cheat, the participants didn't seem to be as influenced by the risk of being caught as one might think. When the students were given the opportunity to cheat without being able to shred their papers, they increased their correct answers from 32.6 to 36.2. But when they were offered the chance to shred their papers—hiding their little crime completely—they didn't push their dishonesty farther. They still cheated at about the same level. This means that even when we have no chance of getting caught, we still don't become wildly dishonest.

When the students could shred both their papers, dip their hand into the money jar, and walk away, every one of them

---

*The distribution of the number of correctly solved questions remained the same across all four conditions, but with a mean shift when the participants could cheat.

could have claimed a perfect test score, or could have taken more money (the jar had about $100 in it). But none of them did. Why? Something held them back—something inside them. But what was it? What is honesty, anyhow?

To THAT QUESTION, Adam Smith, the great economic thinker, had a pleasant reply: "Nature, when she formed man for society, endowed him with an original desire to please, and an original aversion to offend his bretheren. She taught him to feel pleasure in their favourable, and pain in their unfavourable regard," he noted.

To this Smith added, "The success of most people . . . almost always depends upon the favour and good opinion of their neighbours and equals; and without a tolerably regular conduct these can very seldom be obtained. The good old proverb, therefore, that honesty is always the best policy, holds, in such situations, almost always perfectly true."

That sounds like a plausible industrial-age explanation, as balanced and harmonious as a set of balance weights and perfectly meshed gears. However optimistic this perspective might seem, Smith's theory had a darker corollary: since people engage in a cost-benefit analysis with regard to honesty, they can also engage in a cost-benefit analysis to be dishonest. According to this perspective, individuals are honest only to the extent that suits them (including their desire to please others).

Are decisions about honesty and dishonesty based on the same cost-benefit analysis that we use to decide between cars, cheeses, and computers? I don't think so. First of all, can you imagine a friend explaining to you the cost-benefit analysis that went into buying his new laptop? Of course. But can you imagine your friend sharing with you a cost-benefit analysis of the decision regarding stealing a laptop? Of course not—not unless your friend is a professional thief. Rather, I agree with others (from Plato down) who say that honesty is something bigger—something that is considered a moral virtue in nearly every society.

Sigmund Freud explained it this way. He said that as we grow up in society, we internalize the social virtues. This internalization leads to the development of the superego. In general, the superego is pleased when we comply with society's ethics, and unhappy when we don't. This is why we stop our car at four AM when we see a red light, even if we know that no one is around; and it is why we get a warm feeling when we return a lost wallet to its owner, even if our identity is never revealed. Such acts stimulate the reward centers of our brain—the nucleus accumbens and the caudate nucleus—and make us content.

But if honesty is important to us (in a recent survey of nearly 36,000 high school students in the United States, 98 percent of them said it was important to be honest), and if honesty makes us feel good, why are we so frequently dishonest?

This is my take. We care about honesty and we want to be honest. The problem is that our internal honesty monitor is active only when we contemplate big transgressions, like grabbing an entire box of pens from the conference hall. For the little transgressions, like taking a single pen or two pens, we don't even consider how these actions would reflect on our honesty and so our superego stays asleep.

Without the superego's help and monitoring of our honesty, the only defense we have against this kind of transgression is a rational cost-benefit analysis. But who is going to consciously weigh the benefits of taking a towel from a hotel room versus the cost of being caught? Who is going to consider the costs and benefits of adding a few receipts to a tax statement? As we saw in the experiment at Harvard, the cost-benefit analysis, and the probability of getting caught in particular, does not seem to have much influence on dishonesty.

THIS IS THE way the world turns. It's almost impossible to open a newspaper without seeing a report of a dishonest or deceptive act. We watch as the credit card companies bleed their customers with outrageous interest rate hikes; as the airlines plunge into bankruptcy and then call on the federal government to get them—and their underfunded pension funds—out of trouble; and as schools defend the presence of soda machines on campus (and rake in millions from the soft drinks firms) all the while knowing that sugary drinks make kids hyperactive and fat. Taxes are a festival of eroding ethics, as the insightful and talented reporter David Cay Johnston of the *New York Times* describes in *Perfectly Legal: The Covert Campaign to Rig Our Tax System to Benefit the Super Rich—and Cheat Everybody Else* (2005).

Against all of this society, in the form of the government, has battled back, at least to some extent. The Sarbanes-Oxley Act of 2002 (which requires the chief executives of public companies to vouch for the firms' audits and accounts) was passed to make debacles like Enron's a thing of the past. Congress has also passed restrictions on "earmarking" (specifically the pork-barrel spending that politicians insert into larger federal bills). The Securities and Exchange Commission even passed requirements for additional disclosure about executives' pay and perks–so that when we see a stretch limo carrying a Fortune 500 executive, we know pretty certainly how much the corporate chief inside is getting paid.

But can external measures like these really plug all the holes and prevent dishonesty? Some critics say they can't. Take the ethics reforms in Congress, for instance. The statutes ban lobbyists from serving free meals to congressmen and their aides at "widely attended" functions. So what have lobbyists done? Invited congressmen to luncheons with "limited" guest lists that circumvent the rule. Similarly, the new ethics laws ban lobbyists from flying congressmen in "fixed-wing" aircraft. So hey, how about a lift in a helicopter?

The most amusing new law I've heard about is called the "toothpick rule." It states that although lobbyists can no longer provide sit-down meals to congressmen, the lobbyists can still serve anything (presumably hors d'oeuvres) the legislators can stand up and plop into the mouth using their fingers or a toothpick.

Did this change the plans of the seafood industry, which had organized a sit-down pasta and oyster dinner for Washington's legislators (called—you guessed it—"Let the World Be Your Oyster"). Of course not. The seafood lobbyists did drop the pasta dish (messy to fork up with a toothpick), but still fed the congressmen well with freshly opened raw oysters (which the congressmen slurped down standing up).[17]

Sarbanes-Oxley has also being called ineffectual. Some critics say that it's rigid and inflexible, but the loudest outcry is from those who call it ambiguous, inconsistent, inefficient, and outrageously expensive (especially for smaller firms). "It hasn't cleaned up corruption," argued William A. Niskanen, chairman of the Cato Institute; "it has only forced companies to jump through hoops."

So much for enforcing honesty through external controls.

They may work in some cases, but not in others. Could there be a better cure for dishonesty?

BEFORE I EVEN attempt to answer that question, let me describe an experiment we conducted that speaks volumes on the subject. A few years ago Nina, On, and I brought a group of participants together in a lab at UCLA and asked them to take a simple math test. The test consisted of 20 simple problems, each requiring participants to find two numbers that would add up to 10 (see the table). They had five minutes to solve as many of the problems as they could, after which they were entered into a lottery. If they won the lottery, they would receive ten dollars for each problem they solved correctly.

As in our experiment at the Harvard Business School, some of the participants handed in their papers directly to the experimenter. They were our control group. The other participants wrote down on another sheet the number of questions they solved correctly, and then disposed of the originals. These participants, obviously, were the ones with the opportunity to cheat. So, given this opportunity, did these participants cheat? As you may have surmised, they did (but, of course, just by a bit).

LOOK AT YOUR WATCH, NOTE THE TIME, AND START SEARCHING FOR TWO NUMBERS IN THE MATRIX BELOW THAT WILL ADD UP TO TO EXACTLY 10. HOW LONG DID IT TAKE YOU?		
1.69	1.82	2.91
4.67	4.81	3.05
5.82	5.06	4.28
6.36	5.19	4.57

Up to now I have not told you anything new. But the key to this experiment was what preceded it. When the participants first came to the lab, we asked some of them to write down the names of 10 books that they read in high school. The others were asked to write down as many of the Ten Commandments they could recall.* After they finished this part of the experiment, we asked them to continue with the matrix task.

This experimental setup meant that some of the participants were tempted to cheat after recalling 10 books that they read in high school, and some of them were tempted after recalling the Ten Commandments. Who do you think cheated more?

When cheating was *not* possible, our participants, on average, solved 3.1 problems correctly.†

When cheating was possible, the group that recalled 10 books read in high school achieved an average score of 4.1 questions solved (or 33 percent more than those who could not cheat).

But the big question is what happened to the other group—the students who first wrote down the Ten Commandments, than took the test, and then ripped up their worksheets. This, as sportscasters say, was the group to watch. Would they cheat—or would the Ten Commandments have an effect on their integrity? The result surprised even us: the students who had been asked to recall the Ten Commandments had not cheated at all. They averaged three correct answers—the

---

*Do you know the Ten Commandments? If you'd like to test yourself, write them down and compare your list with the list at the end of this chapter. To be sure you have them right, don't just say them to yourself; write them down.
†Can the Ten Commandments raise one's math scores? We used the same two memory tasks with the control condition to test that premise. The performance in the control condition was the same regardless of the type of memory task. So the Commandments do not raise math scores.

same basic score as the group that could not cheat, and one less than those who were able to cheat but had recalled the names of the books.

As I walked home that evening I began to think about what had just happened. The group who listed 10 books cheated. Not a lot, certainly—only to that point where their internal reward mechanism (nucleus accumbens and super-ego) kicked in and rewarded them for stopping.

But what a miracle the Ten Commandments had wrought! We didn't even remind our participants what the Commandments were—we just asked each participant to recall them (and almost none of the participants could recall all 10). We hoped the exercise might invoke the idea of honesty among them. And this was clearly what it did. So, we wondered, what's the big idea in all this? It took us a few weeks to come to some conclusions.

FOR ONE, PERHAPS we could bring the Bible back into public life. If we only want to reduce dishonesty, it might not be a bad idea. Then again, some people might object, on the grounds that the Bible implies an endorsement of a particular religion, or merely that it mixes religion in with the commercial and secular world. But perhaps an oath of a different nature would work. What especially impressed me about the experiment with the Ten Commandments was that the students who could remember only one or two commandments were as affected by them as the students who remembered nearly all ten. This indicated that it was not the Commandments themselves that encouraged honesty, but the mere contemplation of a moral benchmark of some kind.

If that were the case, then we could also use nonreligious

benchmarks to raise the general level of honesty. For instance, what about the professional oaths that doctors, lawyers and others swear to—or used to swear? Could those professional oaths do the trick?

The word *profession* comes from the Latin *professus*, meaning "affirmed publicly." Professions started somewhere deep in the past in religion and then spread to medicine and law. Individuals who had mastered esoteric knowledge, it was said, not only had a monopoly on the practice of that knowledge, but had an obligation to use their power wisely and honestly. The oath—spoken and often written—was a reminder to practitioners to regulate their own behavior, and it also provided a set of rules that had to be followed in fulfilling the duties of their profession.

Those oaths lasted a long time. But then, in the 1960s, a strong movement arose to deregulate the professions. Professions were elitist organizations, it was argued, and needed to be turned out into the light of day. For the legal profession that meant more briefs written in plain English prose, cameras in the courtrooms, and advertising. Similar measures against elitism were applied to medicine and banking, and other professions as well. Much of this could have been beneficial, but something was lost when professions were dismantled. Strict professionalism was replaced by flexibility, individual judgment, the laws of commerce, and the urge for wealth, and with it disappeared the bedrock of ethics and values on which the professions had been built.

A study by the state bar of California in the 1990s, for instance, found that a preponderance of attorneys in California were sick of the decline in honor in their work and "profoundly pessimistic" about the condition of the legal profession. Two-thirds said that lawyers today "compromise their professionalism as a result of economic pressure." Nearly 80 percent said that the bar "fails to adequately punish unethical attorneys." Half said they wouldn't become attorneys if they had it to do over again.[18]

A comparable study by the Maryland Judicial Task Force found similar distress among lawyers in that state. According to Maryland's lawyers, their profession had degenerated so badly that "they were often irritable, short-tempered, argumentative, and verbally abusive" or "detached, withdrawn, preoccupied, or distracted." When lawyers in Virginia were asked whether the increasing problems with professionalism were attributable to "a few bad apples" or to a widespread trend, they overwhelmingly said this was a widespread issue.[19]

Lawyers in Florida have been deemed the worst.[20] In 2003 the Florida bar reported that a "substantial minority" of lawyers were "money-grabbing, too clever, tricky, sneaky, and not trustworthy; who had little regard for the truth or fairness, willing to distort, manipulate, and conceal to win; arrogant, condescending, and abusive." They were also "pompous and obnoxious." What more can I say?

The medical profession has its critics as well. The critics mention doctors who do unnecessary surgeries and other procedures just to boost the bottom line: who order tests at laboratories that are giving them kickbacks, and who lean toward medical tests on equipment that they just happen to own. And what about the influence of the pharmaceutical industry? A friend of mine said he sat waiting for his doctor for an hour recently. During that time, he said, four representatives of drug companies went freely into and out of the office.

You could look at almost any professional group and see

signs of similar problems. How about the Association of Petroleum Geologists, for instance? The image I see is Indiana Jones types, with more interest in discussing Jurassic shale and deltaic deposits than in making a buck. But look deeper and you'll find trouble. "There is unethical behavior going on at a much larger scale than most of us would care to think," one member of the association wrote to her colleagues.[21]

What kind of dishonesty, for goodness sake, could be rife in the ranks of petroleum geologists, you ask? Apparently things like using bootlegged seismic and digital data; stealing maps and materials; and exaggerating the promise of certain oil deposits, in cases where a land sale or investment is being made. "The malfeasance is most frequently of shades of gray, rather than black and white," one petroleum geologist remarked.

But let's remember that petroleum geologists are not alone. This decline in professionalism is everywhere. If you need more proof, consider the debate within the field of professional ethicists, who are called more often than ever before to testify at public hearings and trials, where they may be hired by one party or another to consider issues such as treatment rendered to a patient and the rights of the unborn. Are they tempted to bend to the occasion? Apparently so. "Moral Expertise: A Problem in the Professional Ethics of Professional Ethicists," is the title of one article in an ethics journal.[22] As I said, the signs of erosion are everywhere.

WHAT TO DO? Suppose that, rather than invoking the Ten Commandments, we got into the habit of signing our name to some secular statement—similar to a professional oath— that would remind us of our commitment to honesty. Would a simple oath make a difference, in the way that we saw the Ten Commandments make a difference? We needed to find out—hence our next experiment.

Once again we assembled our groups, this time at MIT. In this study, the first participants took our matrix math test and handed in their answers to the experimenter in the front of the room (who counted how many questions they answered correctly and paid them accordingly). The second group also took the test, but the members of this group were told to fold their answer sheet, keep it in their own possession, and tell the experimenter in the front of the room how many of the problems they got right. The experimenter paid them accordingly, and they were off on their way.

The novel aspect of this experiment had to do with the third group. Before these participants began, each was asked to sign the following statement on the answer sheet: "I understand that this study falls under the MIT honor system." After signing this statement, they continued with the task. When the time had elapsed they pocketed their answer sheets, walked to the front of the room, told the experimenter how many problems they had solved correctly, and were paid accordingly.

What were the results? In the control condition, in which cheating was not possible, participants solved on average three problems. In the second condition, in which the participants could pocket their answers, they solved on average 5.5 problems. What was remarkable was the third situation—in which the participants pocketed their answer sheets, but had also signed the honor code statement. In this case they solved, on average, three problems—exactly the same number as the control group. This outcome was similar to the results we achieved with the Ten Commandments. This is an amazing effect of signing a statement about an honor code, particularly when we take into account that MIT doesn't even have an honor code.

So we learned that students cheat when they have a chance to do so, but they don't cheat as much as they could. Moreover, once they begin thinking about honesty—whether by recalling the Ten Commandments or by signing a simple statement—they stop cheating completely. In other words, when we are removed from any benchmarks of ethical thought, we tend to stray into dishonesty. But if we are reminded of morality at the moment we are tempted, then we are much more likely to be honest.

At present, several state bars and professional organizations are scrambling to shore up their professional ethics. Some are increasing courses in college and graduate schools, and others are requiring brush-up ethics classes. In the legal profession, Judge Dennis M. Sweeney of the Howard County (Maryland) circuit published his own book, *Guidelines for Lawyer Courtroom Conduct*," in which he noted, "Most rules, like these, are simply what our mothers would say a polite and well raised man or woman should do. Since, given their other important responsibilities, our mothers (and yours) cannot be in every courtroom in the State, I offer these rules."

Will such general measures work? Let's remember that lawyers do take an oath when they are admitted to the bar, as doctors take an oath when they enter their profession. But occasional swearing of oaths and occasional statements of adherence to rules are not enough. From our experiments, it is clear that oaths and rules must be recalled at, or just before, the moment of temptation. Also, What is more, time is working against us as we try to curb this problem. As I said in Chapter 4 that when social norms collide with market norms, the social norms go away and the market norms stay. Even if the analogy is not exact, honesty offers a related lesson: once professional ethics (the social norms) have declined, getting them back won't be easy.

THIS DOESN'T MEAN that we shouldn't try. Why is honesty so important? For one thing, let's not forget that the United States holds a position of economic power in the world today partly because it is (or at least is perceived to be) one of the world's most honest nations, in terms of its standards of corporate governance.

In 2006, the United States ranked twentieth in the world in terms of integrity, according to one survey (Finland was first and Haiti last, at number 163). On this basis, I would suspect that people doing business with the United States generally feel they can get a fair deal here. But the fact of the matter is that the United States ranked fourteenth in 2000, before the wave of corporate scandals made the business pages in American newspapers look like a police blotter.[23] We are going down the slippery slope, in other words, not up it, and this can have tremendous long-term costs.

Adam Smith reminded us that honesty really is the best policy, especially in business. To get a glimpse at the other side of that realization—at the downside, in a society without trust—you can take a look at several countries. In China, the word of one person in one region rarely carries to another region. Latin America is full of family-run cartels that hand out loans to relatives (and then fail to cut off credit when the debtor begins to default). Iran is another example of a nation stricken by distrust. An Iranian student at MIT told me that business there lacks a platform of trust. Because of this, no one pays in advance, no one offers credit, and no one is willing to take risks. People must hire within their families, where some level of trust still exists. Would you like to live in such a world? Be careful, because without honesty we might get there faster than you'd imagine.

What can we do to keep our country honest? We can read the Bible, the Koran, or whatever reflects our values, perhaps. We can revive professional standards. We can sign our names to promises that we will act with integrity. Another path is to first recognize that when we get into situations where our personal financial benefit stands in opposition to our moral standards, we are able to "bend" reality, see the world in terms compatible with our selfish interest, and become dishonest. What is the answer, than? If we recognize this weakness, we can try to avoid such situations from the outset. We can prohibit physicians from ordering tests that would benefit them financially; we can prohibit accountants and auditors from functioning as consultants to the same companies; we can bar members of Congress from setting their own salaries, and so on.

But this is not the end of the issue of dishonesty. In the next Chapter 12, I will offer some other suggestions about dishonesty, and some other insights into how we struggle with it.

APPENDIX: CHAPTER 11
The Ten Commandments

I am the Lord your God, you shall have no other gods
    before me.
You shall not take the name of the Lord your God in vain.

Keep holy the Sabbath day.
Honor your father and your mother.
You shall not kill.
You shall not commit adultery.
You shall not steal.
You shall not bear false witness.
You shall not covet your neighbor's wife.
You shall not covet your neighbor's goods.

CHAPTER 12

The Context of Our Character, Part II

Why Dealing with Cash Makes Us More Honest

Many of the dormitories at MIT have common areas, where sit a variety of refrigerators that can be used by the students in the nearby rooms. One morning at about eleven, when most of the students were in class, I slipped into the dorms and, floor by floor, went hunting for all the shared refrigerators that I could find.

When I detected a communal fridge, I inched toward it. Glancing cautiously around, I opened the door, slipped in a six-pack of Coke, and walked briskly away. At a safe distance, I paused and jotted down the time and the location of the fridge where I had left my Cokes.

Over the next few days I returned to check on my Coke cans. I kept a diary detailing how many of them remained in the fridge. As you might expect, the half-life of Coke in a college dorm isn't very long. All of them had vanished within 72 hours. But I didn't always leave Cokes behind. In some of the fridges, I left a plate containing six dollar bills. Would the money disappear faster than the Cokes?

Before I answer that question, let me ask you one. Suppose your spouse calls you at work. Your daughter needs a red pencil for school the next day. "Could you bring one home?" How comfortable would you be taking a red pencil from work for your daughter? Very uncomfortable? Somewhat uncomfortable? Completely comfortable?

Let me ask you another question. Suppose there are no red pencils at work, but you can buy one downstairs for a dime. And the petty cash box in your office has been left open, and no one is around. Would you take 10 cents from the petty cash box for a red pencil? Suppose you didn't have any change and needed the 10 cents. Would you feel comfortable taking it? Would that be OK?

I don't know about you, but while I'd find taking a red pencil from work relatively easy, I'd have a very hard time taking the cash. (Luckily for me, I haven't had to face this issue, since my daughter is not in school yet.)

As it turns out, the students at MIT also felt differently about taking cash. As I mentioned, the cans of Coke quickly disappeared within 72 hours; every one of them was gone. But what a different story with the money! The plates of dollar bills remained untouched for 72 hours, until I removed them from the refrigerators.

So what's going on here?

When we look at the world around us, much of the dishonesty we see involves cheating that is one step removed from cash. Companies cheat with their accounting practices; executives cheat by using backdated stock options; lobbyists cheat by underwriting parties for politicians; drug companies cheat by sending doctors and their wives off on posh vacations. To be sure, these people don't cheat with cold cash (except occasionally). And that's my point: cheating is a lot easier when it's a step removed from money.

Do you think that the architects of Enron's collapse—Kenneth Lay, Jeffrey Skilling, and Andrew Fastow—would have stolen money from the purses of old women? Certainly, they took millions of dollars in pension monies from a lot of old women. But do you think they would have hit a woman with a blackjack and pulled the cash from her fingers? You may disagree, but my inclination is to say no.

So what permits us to cheat when cheating involves non-monetary objects, and what restrains us when we are dealing with money? How does that irrational impulse work?

BECAUSE WE ARE so adept at rationalizing our petty dishonesty, it's often hard to get a clear picture of how nonmonetary objects influence our cheating. In taking a pencil, for example, we might reason that office supplies are part of our overall compensation, or that lifting a pencil or two is what everyone does. We might say that taking a can of Coke from a communal refrigerator from time to time is all right, because, after all, we've all had cans of Coke taken from us. Maybe Lay, Skilling, and Fastow thought that cooking the books at Enron was OK, since it was a temporary measure that could be corrected when business improved. Who knows?

To get at the true nature of dishonesty, then, we needed to develop a clever experiment, one in which the object in question would allow few excuses. We thought about it. Suppose we used a plain poker chip. It was not cash, but neither was it an object with a history, like a Coke or a pencil. Would it give us insight into the cheating process? We weren't sure, but it seemed reasonable; and so, a few years ago, Nina, On, and I gave it a try.

This is what happened. As the students at the MIT cafeteria finished their lunches, we interrupted them to ask whether they would like to participate in a five-minute experiment. All they had to do, we explained, was solve 20 simple math problems (finding two numbers that added up to 10). And for this they would get 50 cents per correct answer.

The experiment began similarly in each case, but ended in one of three different ways. When the participants in the first group finished their tests, they took their worksheets up to the experimenter, who tallied their correct answers and paid them 50 cents for each. The participants in the second group were told to tear up their worksheets, stuff the scraps into their pockets or backpacks, and simply tell the experimenter their score. So far this experiment was similar to the tests of honesty described in Chapter 11.

But the participants in the last group had something significantly different in their instructions. We told them, as we had told the previous group, to tear up the worksheets and simply tell the experimenter how many questions they had answered correctly. But this time, the experimenter wouldn't be giving them cash. Rather, she would give them a poker chip for each question they claimed to have solved. The students would then walk 10 feet across the room to another experimenter, who would exchange each poker chip for 50 cents.

Do you see what we were doing? Would the insertion of a poker chip into the transaction—a piece of valueless, nonmonetary currency—affect the students' honesty? Would the poker chip make the students less honest in tallying their answers than the students who received cash immediately? If so, by how much?

Even we were surprised by the results: The participants in the first group (who had no way to cheat) solved an average of 3.5 questions correctly (they were our control group).

The participants in the second group, who tore up their worksheets, claimed to have correctly solved an average of 6.2 questions. Since we can assume that these students did not become smarter merely by tearing up their worksheets, we can attribute the 2.7 additional questions they claimed to have solved to cheating.

But in terms of brazen dishonesty, the participants in the third group took the cake. They were no smarter than the previous two groups, but they claimed to have solved an average of 9.4 problems—5.9 more than the control group and 3.2 more than the group that merely ripped up the worksheets.

This means that when given a chance to cheat under ordinary circumstances, the students cheated, on average, by 2.7 questions. But when they were given the same chance to cheat but with nonmonetary currency, their cheating increased to 5.9—more than doubling in magnitude. What a difference there is in cheating for money versus cheating for something that is a step away from cash!

If that surprises you, consider this. Of the 2,000 participants in our studies of honesty (described in the previous Chapter 11), only four ever claimed to have solved all the problems. In other words, the rate of "total cheating" was four in 2,000.*

---

*Theoretically, it is possible that some people solved all the problems. But since no one in our experiments claimed to have solved 14, 15, 16, 17, 18, or 19 problems, the likelihood that four of our participants solved 20 is very, very low. For this reason we guess that they cheated.

But in the experiment in which we inserted nonmonetary currency (the poker chip), 24 of the study's 450 participants cheated "all the way." How many of these 24 extreme cheaters were in the condition with money versus the condition with tokens? They were all in the token condition (24 of 150 students cheated "all the way" in this condition; this is equivalent to about 320 per 2,000 participants). This means that the tokens not only "release" people from some of their moral constraints, but for quite a few of them, the extent of the release was so complete that they cheated as much as was possible.

This level of cheating is clearly bad, but it could have been worse. Let's not forget that the poker chips in our experiments were transformed into cash within a matter of seconds. What would the rate of dishonesty have been if the transfer from a nonmonetary token to cash took a few days, weeks, or months (as, for instance, in a stock option)? Would even more people cheat, and to a larger extent?

We have learned that given a chance, people cheat. But what's really odd is that most of us don't see this coming. When we asked students in another experiment to predict if people would cheat more for cash than for tokens, the students said no, the amount of cheating would be the same. After all, they explained, the tokens represented real money— and the tokens were exchanged within seconds for actual cash. And so, they predicted, our participants would treat the chips as real cash.

But how wrong they were! They didn't see how fast we can rationalize our dishonesty when it is one step away from cash. Of course, their blindness is ours as well. Perhaps it's why so much cheating goes on. Perhaps it's why Jeff Skilling, Bernie Ebbers, and the entire roster of executives who have been prosecuted in recent years let themselves, and their companies, slide down the slope.

All of us are vulnerable to this weakness, of course. Think about all the insurance fraud that goes on. It is estimated that when consumers report losses on their homes and cars, they creatively stretch their claims by about 10 percent. (Of course, as soon as you report an exaggerated loss, the insurance company raises your rates, so it becomes tit for tat). Again it is not the case that there are many claims that are completely flagrant, but instead many people who have lost, say, a 27-inch television set report the loss of a 32-inch set; those who have lost a 32-inch set report the loss of a 36-inch set, and so on. These same people would be unlikely to steal money directly from the insurance companies (as tempting as that might sometimes be), but reporting what they no longer have—and increasing its size and value by just a little bit—makes the moral burden easier to bear.

There are other interesting practices. Have you ever heard the term "wardrobing"? Wardrobing is buying an item of clothing, wearing it for a while, and then returning it in such a state that the store has to accept it but can no longer resell it. By engaging in wardrobing, consumers are not directly stealing money from the company; instead, it is a dance of buying and returning, with many unclear transactions involved. But there is at least one clear consequence—the clothing industry estimates that its annual losses from wardrobing are about $16 billion (about the same amount as the estimated annual loss from home burglaries and automobile theft combined).

And how about expense reports? When people are on

business trips, they are expected to know what the rules are, but expense reports too are one step, and sometimes even a few steps, removed from cash. In one study, Nina and I found that not all expenses are alike in terms of people's ability to justify them as business expenses. For example, buying a mug for five dollars for an attractive stranger was clearly out of bounds, but buying the same stranger an eight-dollar drink in a bar was very easy to justify. The difference was not the cost of the item, or the fear of getting caught, but people's ability to justify the item to themselves as a legitimate use of their expense account.

A few more investigations into expense accounts turned up similar rationalizations. In one study, we found that when people give receipts to their administrative assistants to submit, they are then one step removed from the dishonest act, and hence more likely to slip in questionable receipts. In another study, we found that businesspeople who live in New York are more likely to consider as a gift for their kid a business expense if they purchased it at the San Francisco airport (or someplace else far from home) than if they had purchased it at the New York airport, or on their way back home from the airport. None of this makes logical sense, but when the medium of exchange is nonmonetary, our ability to rationalize increases by leaps and bounds.

I HAD MY own experience with dishonesty a few years ago. Someone broke into my Skype account (very cool online telephone software) and charged my Paypal account (an online payment system) a few hundred dollars for the service.

I don't think the person who did this was a hardened criminal. From a criminal's perspective, breaking into my account would most likely be a waste of time and talent because if this person was sufficiently smart to hack into Skype, he could probably have hacked into Amazon, Dell, or maybe even a credit card account, and gotten much more value for his time. Rather, I imagine that this person was a smart kid who had managed to hack into my account and who took advantage of this "free" communication by calling anyone who would talk to him, until I managed to regain control over my account. He may have even seen this as a techie challenge—or maybe he is a student to whom I once a bad grade and who decided to tweak my nose for it.

Would this kid have taken cash from my wallet, even if he knew for sure that no one would ever catch him? Maybe, but I suspect that the answer is no. There were some aspects of Skype and of how my account was set up that "helped" this person engage in this activity and not feel morally reprehensible: First, he stole calling time, not money. Next, he did not gain anything tangible from the transaction. Third, he stole from Skype rather than directly from me. Fourth, he might have imagined that at the end of the day Skype, not I, would cover the cost. Fifth, the cost of the calls was charged automatically to me via Paypal. So here we had another step in the process—and another level of fuzziness in terms of who would eventually pay for the calls. (Just in case you are wondering, I have since canceled this direct link to PayPal.)

Was this person stealing from me? Sure, but there were so many things that made the theft fuzzy. I really don't think he thought of himself as a dishonest guy. No cash was taken, right? And was anyone really hurt? This kind of thinking is worrisome. If my problem with Skype was indeed due to the nonmonetary nature of the transactions on Skype, this would mean that there is much more at risk here, including a wide range of online services, and perhaps even credit and debit cards. All these electronic transactions, with no physical exchange of money from hand to hand, might make it easier for people to be dishonest—without ever questioning or fully acknowledging the immorality of their actions.

THERE'S ANOTHER, SINISTER impression that I took out of our studies. In our experiments, the participants were smart, caring, honorable individuals, who for the most part had a clear limit to the amount of cheating they would undertake, even with nonmonetary currency like the poker chips. For almost all of them, there was a point at which their conscience called for them to stop, and they did. Accordingly, the dishonesty that we saw in our experiments was probably the lower boundary of human dishonesty: the level of dishonesty practiced by individuals who want to be ethical and who want to see themselves as ethical—the so-called good people.

The scary thought is that if we did the experiments with nonmonetary currencies that were not as immediately convertible into money as poker chips, or with individuals who cared less about their honesty, or with behavior that was not so publicly observable, we would most likely have found higher levels of dishonesty. In other words, the level of deception we observed here is probably an underestimation of the level of deception we would find in the real world.

Now suppose that you have a company or a division of a company led by a Gordon Gekko character who declares that "greed is good." And suppose he used nonmonetary means of encouraging dishonesty. Can you see how such a swashbuckler could change the mind-set of people who in principle want to be honest and want to see themselves as honest, but also want to hold onto their jobs and get ahead in the world? It is under just such circumstances that nonmonetary currencies can lead us astray. They let us bypass our conscience and freely explore the benefits of dishonesty.

This view of reality is worrisome. We can hope to surround ourselves with good, moral people, but we have to be realistic. Even good people are not immune to being partially blinded by their own minds. This blindness allows them to take actions that bypass their own moral standards on the road to financial rewards. In essence, motivation can play tricks on us whether or not we are good, moral people.

As the author and journalist Upton Sinclair once noted, "It is difficult to get a man to understand something when his salary depends upon his not understanding it." We can now add the following thought: it is even more difficult to get a man to understand something when he is dealing with nonmonetary currencies.

THE PROBLEMS OF dishonesty, by the way, don't apply just to individuals. In recent years we have seen business in general succumb to a lower standard of honesty. I'm not talking about big acts of dishonesty, like those perpetrated by Enron and Worldcom. I mean the small acts of dishonesty that are similar to swiping Cokes out of the refrigerator. There are companies out there, in other words, that aren't stealing cash off our plates, so to speak, but are stealing things one step removed from cash.

There are plenty of examples. Recently, one of my friends, who had carefully saved up his frequent-flyer miles for a vacation, went to the airline who issued all these miles. He was told that all the dates he wanted were blacked out. In other words, although he had saved up 25,000 frequent-flyer miles, he couldn't use them (and he tried many dates). But, the representative said, if he wanted to use 50,000 miles, there might be some seats. She checked. Sure, there were seats everywhere.

To be sure, there was probably some small print in the frequently-flyer brochure explaining that this was OK. But to my friend, the 25,000 miles he had earned represented a lot of money. Let's say it was $450. Would this airline have mugged him for that amount of cash? Would the airline have swiped it from his bank account? No. But because it was one step removed, the airline stole it from him in the form of requiring 25,000 additional miles.

For another example, look at what banks are doing with credit card rates. Consider what is called two-cycle billing. There are several variations of this trick, but the basic idea is that the moment you don't pay your bill in full, the credit issuer will not only charge a high interest rate on new purchases, but will actually reach into the past and charge interest on past purchases as well. When the Senate banking committee looked into this recently, it heard plenty of testimony that certainly made the banks look dishonest. For instance, a man in Ohio who charged $3,200 to his card soon found his debt to be $10,700 because of penalties, fees, and interest.

These were not boiler-room operators charging high interest rates and fees, but some of the biggest and presumably most reputable banks in America—those whose advertising campaigns would make you believe that you and the bank were "family." Would a family member steal your wallet? No. But these banks, with a transaction somewhat removed from cash, apparently would.

Once you view dishonesty through this lens, it is clear that you can't open a newspaper in the morning without seeing new examples to add.

AND SO WE return to our original observation: isn't cash strange? When we deal with money, we are primed to think about our actions as if we had just signed an honor code. If you look at a dollar bill, in fact, it seems to have been designed to conjure up a contract: the united states of america, it says in prominent type, with a shadow beneath that makes it seem three-dimensional. And there is George Washington himself (and we all know that he could never tell a lie). And then, on the back, it gets even more serious: in god we trust, it says. And then we've got that weird pyramid, and on top, that unblinking eye! And it's looking right at us! In addition to all this symbolism, the sanctity of money could also be aided by the fact that money is a clear unit of exchange. It's hard to say that a dime is not a dime, or a buck isn't a buck.

But look at the latitude we have with nonmonetary exchanges. There's always a convenient rationale. We can take a pencil from work, a Coke from the fridge—we can even backdate our stock options—and find a story to explain it all. We can be dishonest without thinking of ourselves as dishonest. We can steal while our conscience is apparently fast asleep.

How can we fix this? We could label each item in the supply cabinet with a price, for instance, or use wording that explains stocks and stock options clearly in terms of their monetary value. But in the larger context, we need to wake up to the connection between nonmonetary currency and

229

our tendency to cheat. We need to recognize that once cash is a step away, we will cheat by a bigger factor than we could ever imagine. We need to wake up to this—individually and as a nation, and do it soon.

Why? For one thing, the days of cash are coming to a close. Cash is a drag on the profits of banks—they want to get rid of it. On the other hand, electronic instruments are very profitable. Profits from credit cards in the United States rose from $9 billion in 1996 to a record $27 billion in 2004. By 2010, banking analysts say, there will be $50 billion in new electronic transactions, nearly twice the number processed under the Visa and MasterCard brands in 2004.[24] The question, therefore, is how we can control our tendency to cheat when we are brought to our senses only by the sight of cash—and what we can do now that cash is going away.

Willie Sutton once said that he robbed banks because that's where the money was. By that logic he might be writing the fine print for a credit card company today or penciling in blackout dates for an airline. It might not be where the cash is, but it's certainly where you will find the money.

CHAPTER 13

Beer and Free Lunches

*What Is Behavioral Economics, and Where
Are the Free Lunches?*

The Carolina Brewery is a hip bar on Franklin Street, the main street outside the University of North Carolina at Chapel Hill. A beautiful street with brick buildings and old trees, it has many restaurants, bars, and coffee shops—more than one would expect to find in a small town.

As you open the doors to the Carolina Brewery, you see an old building with high ceilings and exposed beams, and a few large stainless steel beer containers that promise a good time. There are semiprivate tables scattered around. This is a favorite place for students as well as an older crowd to enjoy good beer and food.

Soon after I joined MIT, Jonathan Levav (a professor at Columbia) and I were mulling over the kinds of questions one might conjure up in such a pleasant pub. First, does the sequential process of taking orders influence the choices that the people sitting around the table ultimately make? In other words, are the patrons influenced by the selections of the others around them? Second, if this is the case, does it encourage conformity or nonconformity? In other words, would the patrons sitting around a table intentionally choose beers that were different from or the same as the choices of the others? Finally, we wanted to know whether being influenced by others' choices would make people better or worse off, in terms of how much they enjoyed their beer.

THROUGHOUT THIS BOOK, I have described experiments that I hoped would be surprising and illuminating. If they were, it was largely because they refuted the common assumption that we are all fundamentally rational. Time and again I have provided examples that are contrary to Shakespeare's depiction of us in "What a piece of work is a man." In fact, we are not noble in reason, not infinite in faculty, and rather weak in apprehension. (Frankly, I think Shakespeare knew that very well, and this speech of Hamlet's is not without irony.)

In this final chapter, I will present an experiment that offers one more example of our predictable irrationality. Then I will further describe the general economic perspective on human behavior, contrast it with behavioral economics, and draw some conclusions. Let me begin with the experiment.

TO GET TO the bottom of the sudsy barrel of questions that we thought of at the Carolina Brewery, Jonathan and I decided to plunge in—metaphorically, of course. We started by asking the manager of the Carolina Brewery to let us to serve free samples of beer to the customers—as long as we paid for the beer ourselves. (Imagine how difficult it was, later, to convince the MIT accountants that a $1,400 bill for beer is a legitimate research expense.) The manager of the bar was happy to comply. After all, he would sell us the beer and his customers would receive a free sample, which would presumably increase their desire to return to the brewery.

Handing us our aprons, he established his one and only condition: that we approach the people and get their orders for samples within one minute of the time they sat down. If we couldn't make it in time, we would indicate this to the regular waiters and they would approach the table and take the orders. This was reasonable. The manager didn't know how efficient we could be as waiters, and he didn't want to delay the service by too much. We started working.

I approached a group as soon as they had sat down. They seemed to be undergraduate couples on a double date. Both guys were wearing what looked like their best slacks, and the girls had on enough makeup to make Elizabeth Taylor look unadorned in comparison. I greeted them, offered them the free sample, and then proceeded to describe the four beers:

1) Coppeline Amber Ale: A medium-bodied red ale with a well-balanced hop and malt character and a traditional ale fruitiness.
2) Franklin Street Lager: A Bohemian pilsner-style golden lager brewed with a soft maltiness and a crisp hoppy finish.
3) India Pale Ale: A well-hopped robust ale originally brewed to withstand the long ocean journey from England around the cape of Africa to India. It is dry-hopped with cascade hops for a fragrant floral finish.
4) Summer Wheat Ale: Bavarian-style ale, brewed with 50 percent wheat as a light, spritzy, refreshing summer

drink. It is gently hopped and has a unique aroma reminiscent of banana and clove from an authentic German yeast strain.

Which would you choose?

☐ Coppeline Amber Ale
☐ Franklin Street Lager
☐ India Pale Ale
☐ Summer Wheat Ale

After describing the beers, I asked one of the guys—the blond-haired guy—and asked for his selection; he chose the India Pale Ale. The girl with the more elaborate hairdo was next; she chose the Franklin Street Lager. Then I turned to the other girl. She opted for the Copperline Amber Ale. Her boyfriend, who was last, selected the Summer Wheat Ale. With their orders in hand, I rushed to the bar, where Bob— the tall, handsome bartender, a senior in computer science— stood smiling. Aware that we were in a hurry, he filled my order before any of the others. I then took the tray with the four two-ounce samples back to the double-daters' table and placed their beers in front of them.

Along with their samples, I handed each of them a short survey, printed on the brewery's stationery. In this survey we asked the respondents how much they liked their beer and whether they had regretted choosing a particular brand. After I collected their surveys, I continued to observe the four people from a distance to see whether any of them took a sip of anyone else's beer. As it turned out, none of them shared a sample.

Jonathan and I repeated this procedure with 49 more tables. Then we continued, but for the next 50 tables we changed the procedure. This time, after we read the descriptions of the beers, we handed the participants a small menu with the names of the four beers and asked each of them to write down their preferred beer, rather than just saying it. In so doing, we transformed ordering from a public event into a private one. This meant that each participant would not hear what the others—including, perhaps, someone they were trying hard to impress—ordered and so could not be influenced by it.

What happened? We found that when people order out loud in sequence, they choose differently from when they order in private. When ordering sequentially, they order more different brands of beers per table—in essence opting for variety. A basic way to understand this is the Summer Wheat Ale was not very attractive, but when the other beers were "taken," our participants felt that they had to choose something different—perhaps to show that they had a mind of their own and weren't trying to copy the others—and so they chose another beer, one that they may not have initially wanted, but one that conveyed their individuality.

What about their enjoyment of the beer? It stands to reason that if people choose beer that nobody has chosen just to convey uniqueness, they will probably end up with a beer that they don't really want or like. And indeed this was the case. Overall, those who made their choices out loud, in the standard way that food is ordered at restaurants, were not as happy as those who made their choices privately, without taking others' opinions into consideration. There was, however, one very important exception: the first person to order beer in the group that made its decisions out loud was de facto in the same condition as the people who expressed their opinion privately, since he or she was unencumbered, in choosing, by other people's choices. Accordingly, we found that the first person to order beer in the sequential group was the happiest of the group and just as happy as those who chose their beers in private.

BY THE WAY, a funny thing happened when we ran the experiment in the Carolina Brewery: Dressed in my waiter's outfit, I approached one of the tables and began to read the menu to the couple there. Suddenly, I realized that the man was Rick, a graduate student in computer science, someone with whom I had worked on a project related to computational vision three or four years earlier. Because the experiment had to be conducted in the same way each time, this was not a good time for me to chat with him, so I put on a poker face and launched into a matter-of-fact description of the beers. After I finished, Rick stopped me to ask how I was doing:

"Very well, thank you," I said. "Which of the beers can I get you?"

He and his companion both selected beers, and then Rick took another stab at conversation: "Dan, did you ever finish you PhD?"

"Yes," I said, "I finished about a year ago. Excuse me; I will be right back with your beers." As I walked to the bar to fill their order, I realized that Rick must have thought that this was my profession and that a degree in social science would only get someone a job as a beer server. When I got back to the table with the samples, Rick and his companion—who was his wife—tasted the beers and answered the short questionnaire. Then Rick tried again. He told me that he had recently read one of my papers and liked it a lot. It was a good paper, and I liked it too, but I think he was just trying to make me feel better about my job as a beer server.

ANOTHER STUDY, CONDUCTED later at Duke with wine samples and MBA students, allowed us to measure some of the participants' personality traits—something that the manager of the Carolina Brewery had not been thrilled about. This opened the door for us to find out what might be contributing to an interesting phenomenon. What we found was a correlation between the tendency to order alcoholic beverages that were different from what other people at the table had chosen and a personality trait called "need for uniqueness." In essence, individuals more concerned with portraying their own uniqueness were more likely to order an alcoholic beverage not yet ordered in an effort to demonstrate that they were in fact one of a kind.

What these results show is that people are sometimes willing to sacrifice the pleasure they get from a particular consumption experience in order to project a certain image to others. When people order food and drinks, they seem to have two goals: to order what they will enjoy most and to portray themselves in a positive light in the eyes of their friends. The problem is that once they order, say, the food, they may be stuck with a dish they don't like—a situation they often regret. In essence people, particularly those with a high need for uniqueness, may sacrifice personal utility in order to gain reputational utility.

Although these results were clear, we suspected that in other cultures—where the need for uniqueness is not considered a positive trait—people who ordered aloud in public would try to portray a sense of belonging to the group and express more conformity in their choices. In a study we conducted in Hong Kong, we found that this was indeed the case. In Hong Kong, individuals also selected food that they did not like as much when they selected it in public rather than in private, but these participants chose the same item as the first person in the group selected—again making a regrettable mistake, though a different type of mistake, when ordering food.

FROM WHAT I have told you so far about this experiment, you can see that a bit of simple life advice—a free lunch—comes out of this research. First, when you go to a restaurant, it's a good idea to plan your order before the waiter approaches you, and stick to it. Being swayed by what other people choose might lead you to choose a worse alternative. If you're afraid that you might be swayed anyway, a useful strategy is to announce your order to the table before the waiter comes. This way, you have staked a claim to your order, and it's less likely that other people, even someone ordering before you, will take what you have selected. But of course the best option is to order first.

Perhaps restaurant owners should ask their customers to write out orders privately, so that no customer will be influenced by the orders of his or her companions. We pay a lot of money for the pleasure of dining out. This is most likely the cheapest and simplest way to increase the enjoyment derived from dining out.

But there's a bigger lesson that I would like to draw from this experiment—and in fact from all that I have said in the preceding chapters. Standard economics assumes that we are rational—that we know all the pertinent information about our decisions, that we can calculate the value of the different options we face, and that we are cognitively unhindered in weighing the ramifications of each potential choice.

The result is that we are presumed to be making logical and sensible decisions. And even if we make a wrong decision from time to time, the standard economics perspective suggests that we will quickly learn from our mistakes either on our own or with the help of "market forces." On the basis of these assumptions, economists draw far-reaching conclusions about everything from shopping trends to law to public policy.

But, as the results presented in this book (and others) show, we are all far less rational in our decision making than standard economic theory assumes. Our irrational behaviors are neither random nor senseless—they are systematic and predictable. We all make the same types of mistakes over and over, because of the basic wiring of our brains. So wouldn't it make sense to modify standard economics and move away from naive psychology, which often fails the tests of reason, introspection, and—most important—empirical scrutiny?

Wouldn't economics make a lot more sense if it were based on how people actually behave, instead of how they should behave? As I said in the Introduction, that simple idea is the basis of behavioral economics, an emerging field focused on the (quite intuitive) idea that people do not always behave rationally and that they often make mistakes in their decisions. The research described in this book is but a small part of this emerging field.

In many ways, the standard economic and Shakespearian views are more optimistic about human nature, since they assume that our capacity for reasoning is limitless. By the same token the behavioral economics view, which acknowledges human deficiencies, is more depressing, because it demonstrates the many ways in which we fall short of our ideals. Indeed, it can be rather depressing to realize that we all continually make irrational decisions in our personal, professional, and social lives. But there is a silver lining: the fact that we make mistakes also means that there are ways to improve our decisions—and therefore that there are opportunities for "free lunches."

ONE OF THE main differences between standard and behavioral economics involves this concept of "free lunches." According to the assumptions of standard economics, all human decisions are rational and informed, motivated by an accurate concept of the worth of all goods and services and the amount of happiness (utility) all decisions are likely to produce. Under this set of assumptions, everyone in the marketplace is trying to maximize profit and striving to optimize his experiences. As a consequence, economic theory asserts that there are no free lunches—if there were any, someone would have already found them and extracted all their value.

Behavioral economists, on the other hand, believe that people are susceptible to irrelevant influences from their immediate environment (which we call context effects), irrelevant emotions, shortsightedness, and other forms of irrationality (see any chapter in this book for more examples). What good news can accompany this realization? The good news is that these mistakes also provide opportunities for improvement. If we all make systematic mistakes in our decisions, then why not develop new strategies, tools, and methods to help us make better decisions and improve our overall well-being? That's exactly the meaning of free lunches from the perspective of behavioral economics—the idea that there are tools, methods, and policies that can help all of us make better decisions and as a consequence achieve what we desire.

For example, why Americans are not saving enough for retirement is a meaningless question from the perspective of standard economics. If we are all making good, informed decisions in every aspect of our lives, then we are also saving the exact amount that we want to save. We might not save much because we don't care about the future, because we are looking forward to experiencing poverty at retirement, because we expect our kids to take care of us, or because we are hoping to win the lottery—there are many possible reasons. The main point is that from the standard economic perspective, we are saving exactly the right amount in accordance with our preferences.

But from the perspective of behavioral economics, which does not assume that people are rational, the idea that we are not saving enough is perfectly reasonable. In fact, research in behavioral economics points to many possible reasons why people are not saving enough for retirement. People procrastinate. People have a hard time understanding the real cost of not saving as well as the benefits of saving. (By how much would your life be better in the future if you were to deposit an additional $1,000 in your retirement account every month for the next 20 years?) Being "house rich" helps people believe that they are indeed rich. It is easy to create consumption habits and hard to give them up. And there are many, many more reasons.

The potential for free lunches from the perspective of behavioral economics lies in new methods, mechanisms, and other interventions that would help people achieve more of what they truly want. For example, the new and innovative credit card that I described in Chapter 6, on self-control, could help people exercise more self-control within the domain of spending. Another example of this approach is a mechanism called "save more tomorrow," which Dick Thaler and Shlomo Benartzi proposed and tested a few years ago.

Here's how "save more tomorrow" works. When new employees join a company, in addition to the regular decisions they are asked to make about what percentage of their paycheck to invest in their company's retirement plan, they are also asked what percentage of their future salary raises they would be willing to invest in the retirement plan. It is difficult to sacrifice consumption today for saving in the distant future, but it is psychologically easier to sacrifice consumption in the future, and even easier to give up a percentage of a salary increase that one does not yet have.

When the plan was implemented in Thaler and Benartzi's test, the employees joined and agreed to have their contribution, as a percentage, increase with their future salary raises. What was the outcome? Over the next few years, as the employees received raises, the saving rates increased from about 3.5 percent to around 13.5 percent—a gain for the employees, their families, and the company, which by now had more satisfied and less worried employees.

This is the basic idea of free lunches—providing benefits for all the parties involved. Note that these free lunches don't have to be without cost (implementing the self-control credit card or "save more tomorrow" inevitably involves a cost). As long as these mechanisms provide more benefits than costs, we should consider them to be free lunches—mechanisms that provide net benefits to all parties.

IF I WERE to distill one main lesson from the research described in this book, it is that we are pawns in a game whose forces we largely fail to comprehend. We usually think of ourselves as sitting in the driver's seat, with ultimate control over the decisions we make and the direction our life takes; but, alas, this perception has more to do with our desires— with how we want to view ourselves—than with reality.

Each of the chapters in this book describes a force (emotions, relativity, social norms, etc.) that influences our behavior. And while these influences exert a lot of power over our behavior, our natural tendency is to vastly underestimate this power. These influences have an effect not because we lack knowledge, lack practice, or are weak-minded. On the contrary, they repeatedly affect experts as well as novices in systematic and predictable ways. The resulting mistakes are simply how we go about our lives, how we "do business." They are a part of us.

Visual illusions are also illustrative here. Just as we can't help being fooled by visual illusions, we fall for the "decision illusions" our minds show us. The point is that our visual and decision environments are filtered to us courtesy of our eyes, our ears, our senses of smell and touch, and the master of it all, our brain. By the time we comprehend and digest information, it is not necessarily a true reflection of reality. Instead, it is our representation of reality, and this is the input we base our decisions on. In essence we are limited to the tools nature has given us, and the natural way in which we make decisions is limited by the quality and accuracy of these tools.

A second main lesson is that although irrationality is commonplace, it does not necessarily mean that we are helpless. Once we understand when and where we may make erroneous decisions, we can try to be more vigilant, force ourselves to think differently about these decisions, or use technology to overcome our inherent shortcomings. This is also where businesses and policy makers could revise their thinking and consider how to design their policies and products so as to provide free lunches.

THANK YOU FOR reading this book. I hope you have learned some interesting ideas about human behavior, gained some insight into what really makes us tick, and discovered ways to improve your decision making. I also hope that I have been able to share with you my enthusiasm for the study of rationality and irrationality. In my opinion, studying human behavior is a fantastic gift because it helps us better understand ourselves and the daily mysteries we encounter. And although the topic is important and fascinating, it is not easy to study, and there is still a lot of work ahead of us. As the Nobel laureate Murray Gell-Mann once said, "Think how hard physics would be if particles could think."

Irrationally yours,
Dan Ariely

PS: If you want to participate in this journey, log on to *www.predictablyirrational.com,* sign up for a few of our studies, and leave us your ideas and thoughts.

Thanks

Over the years I have been fortunate to work on joint research projects with smart, creative, generous individuals. The research described in this book is largely an outcome of their ingenuity and insight, but also of their lack of judgment—mostly evident when they agreed to work with me on these projects. These individuals are not only great researchers, but also close friends. They made this research possible. Any mistakes and omissions in this book are mine. (Short biographies of these wonderful researchers follow.)

Much of the research described in this book was carried out while I was at MIT, and many of the participants and research assistants were MIT students. The results of the experiments highlight their (as well as our own) irrationalities, and sometimes poke fun at them, but this should not be confused with a lack of caring or a lack of admiration. These students are extraordinary in their motivation, love of learning, curiosity, and generous spirit. It has been a privilege to get to know you all—you even made Boston's winters worthwhile!

I also want to add a special word of thanks to the administration at MIT: for showing me new heights of irrationality, and that life can indeed look like an episode of the BBC comedy series *Yes Minister*.

Figuring out how to write in "non-academese" was not easy, but I got a lot of help along the way. My deepest thanks to Jim Levine, Lindsay Edgecombe, Elizabeth Fisher, and the incredible team at the Levine Greenberg Literary Agency. I am also indebted to Sandy Blakeslee for her insightful advice; and to Rebecca Waber, Ania Jakubek, Carlie Burck, Bronwyn Fryer, Devra Nelson, Janelle Stanley, Michal Strahilevitz, and Ellen Hoffman for their role in helping me translate some of these ideas into words. Special thanks to my writing partner, Erik Calonius, who contributed many of the real-world examples that you will read in these pages, with a style that helped me tell this story as well as it could be told. Special thanks also go to my trusting, supporting, and helpful editor at HarperCollins, Claire Wachtel.

I wrote the book while visiting the Institute for Advanced Study at Princeton. I cannot imagine a more ideal environment in which to think and write. I even got to spend some time in the institute's kitchen, learning to chop, bake, sauté, and cook under the supervision of chefs Michel Reymond and Yann Blanchet—I couldn't have asked for a better place to expand my horizons.

Finally, thanks to my lovely wife Sumi, who has had to listen to my research stories over and over and over and over. And while I hope you agree that they are somewhat amusing

for the first few reads, her patience and willingness to repeatedly lend me her ear merits sainthood. Sumi, tonight I will be
home at seven-fifteen at the latest; make it eight o'clock,
maybe eight-thirty; I promise.

List of Collaborators

On Amir
On joined MIT as a PhD student a year after me and became "my" first student. As my first student, On had a tremendous role in shaping what I expect from students and how I see our relationship. In addition to being exceptionally smart, On has an amazing set of skills, and what he does not know he is able to learn within a day or two. It is always exciting to work and spend time with him. On is currently a professor at the University of California at San Diego.

Marco Bertini
When I first met Marco, he was a PhD student at Harvard Business School, and unlike his fellow students he did not see the Charles River as an obstacle he should not cross. Marco is Italian, with a temperament and sense of style to match— an overall great guy you just want to go out for a drink with. Marco is currently a professor at London Business School.

Ziv Carmon

Ziv was one of the main reasons I joined Duke's PhD program, and the years we spent together at Duke justified this decision. Not only did I learn from him a great deal about decision making and how to conduct research; he also became one of my dear friends, and the advice I got from him over the years has repeatedly proved to be invaluable. Ziv is currently a professor at INSEAD's Singapore campus.

Shane Frederick

I met Shane while I was a student at Duke and he was a student at Carnegie Mellon. We had a long discussion about fish over sushi, and this has imprinted on me a lasting love for both. A few years later Shane and I both moved to MIT and had many more opportunities for sushi and lengthy discussions, including the central question of life: "If a bat and a ball cost $1.10 in total, and the bat costs a dollar more than the ball, how much does the ball cost?" Shane is currently a professor at MIT.

James Heyman

James and I spent a year together at Berkeley. He would often come in to discuss some idea bearing on one of his recent baking outputs, and this was always a good start for an interesting discussion. Following his life's maxim that money isn't everything, his research focuses on nonfinancial aspects of marketplace transactions. One of James's passions is the many ways behavioral economics could play out in policy decisions, and over the years I have come to see the wisdom in this approach. James is currently a professor at the University of St. Thomas (in Minnesota, not the Virgin Islands).

Leonard Lee

Leonard joined the PhD program at MIT to work on related economics topics. Since we both kept long hours, we started taking breaks together late at night, and this gave us a chance to start working jointly on a few research projects. The collaboration with Leonard has been great. He has endless energy and enthusiasm, and the number of experiments he can carry out during an average week is about what other people need a semester for. In addition, he is one of the nicest people I have ever met and always a delight to chat and work with. Leonard is currently a professor at Columbia University

Jonathan Levav

Jonathan loves his mother like no one else I have met, and his main regret in life is that he disappointed her when he didn't go to medical school. Jonathan is smart, funny, and an incredibly social animal, able to make new friends in fractions of seconds. He is physically big with a large head, large teeth, and an even larger heart. Jonathan is currently a professor at Columbia University.

George Loewenstein

George is one of my first, favorite, and longest-time collaborators. He is also my role model. In my mind George is the most creative and broadest researcher in behavioral economics. George has an incredible ability to observe the world around him and find nuances of behavior that are important for our understanding of human nature as well as for policy. George is currently, and appropriately, the Herbert A. Simon Professor of Economics and Psychology at Carnegie Mellon University.

Nina Mazar

Nina first came to MIT for a few days to get feedback on her research and ended up staying for five years. During this time we had oodles of fun working together and I came to greatly rely on her. Nina is oblivious of obstacles, and her willingness to take on large challenges led us to carry out some particularly difficult experiments in rural India. For many years I hoped that she would never decide to leave; but, alas, at some point the time came: she is currently a professor at the University of Toronto. In an alternative reality, Nina is a high-fashion designer in Milan, Italy.

Elie Ofek

Elie is an electrical engineer by training who then saw the light (or so he believes) and switched to marketing. Not surprisingly, his main area of research and teaching is innovations and high-tech industries. Elie is a great guy to have coffee with because he has interesting insights and perspectives on every topic. Currently, Elie is a professor at Harvard Business School (or as its members call it, "The Haaarvard Business School.")

Yesim Orhun

Yesim is a true delight in every way. She is funny, smart, and sarcastic. Regrettably, we had only one year to hang out while we were both at Berkeley. Yesim's research takes findings from behavioral economics and, using this starting point, provides prescriptions for firms and policy makers. For some odd reason, what really gets her going is any research question that includes the words *simultaneity* and *endogeneity*. Yesim is currently a professor at the University of Chicago.

Drazen Prelec

Drazen is one of the smartest people I have ever met and one of the main reasons I joined MIT. I think of Drazen as academic royalty: he knows what he is doing, he is sure of himself, and everything he touches turns to gold. I was hoping that by osmosis, I would get some of his style and depth, but having my office next to his was not sufficient for this. Drazen is currently a professor of management science at MIT.

Kristina Shampanier

Kristina came to MIT to be trained as an economist, and for some odd but wonderful reason elected to work with me. Kristina is exceptionally smart, and I learned a lot from her over the years. As a tribute to her wisdom, when she graduated from MIT, she opted for a nonacademic job: she is now a high-powered consultant in Boston.

Jiwoong Shin

Jiwoong's is a yin and yang researcher. On one hand he carries out research in standard economics assuming that individuals are perfectly rational; and on the other hand he carries out research in behavioral economics showing that people are irrational. He is thoughtful and reflective—a philosophical type—and this duality does not faze him. Jiwoong and I started working together mostly because we wanted to have fun together, and indeed we have spent many exciting hours working together. Jiwoong is currently a professor at Yale University.

Baba Shiv

Baba and I first met when we were both PhD students at Duke. Over the years Baba has carried out fascinating research in many areas of decision making, particularly on how emotions influence decision making. He is terrific in every way and the kind of person who makes everything around him seem magically better. Baba is currently a professor at Stanford University.

Rebecca Waber

Rebecca is one of the most energetic and happiest people I have ever met. She is also the only person I ever observed to burst out laughing while reading her marriage vows. Rebecca is particularly interested in research on decision making applied to medical decisions, and I count myself as very lucky that she chose to work with me on these topics. Rebecca is currently a graduate student at the Media Laboratory at MIT.

Klaus Wertenbroch

Klaus and I met when he was a starting professor at Duke and I was a PhD student. Klaus's interest in decision making is mostly based on his attempts to make sense of his own deviation from rationality, whether it is his smoking habit or his procrastination in delaying work for the pleasure of watching soccer on television. It was only fitting that we worked together on procrastination. Klaus is currently a professor at INSEAD.

Bibliography and Additional Readings

Below is a list of the papers on which the chapters were based, plus suggestions for additional readings on each topic.

Chapter 1: The Truth about Relativity

BASED ON

Amos Tversky and Daniel Kahneman, "The Framing of Decisions and The psychology of Choice," *Science* (1981).

RELATED READINGS

Joel Huber, John Payne, and Chris Puto, "Adding Asymmetrically Dominated Alternatives: Violations of Regularity and the Similarity Hypothesis," *Journal of Consumer Research*, (1982).

Itamar Simonson, "Choice Based on Reasons: The Case of Attraction and Compromise Effects," *Journal of Consumer Research* (1989).

Amos Tversky and Itamar Simonson, "Context-Dependent Preferences," *Management Science* (1993).

Dan Ariely and Tom Wallsten, "Seeking Subjective Dominance in Multidimensional Space: An Explanation of the Asymmetric Dominance Effect," *Organizational Behavior and Human Decision Processes* (1995).

Constantine Sedikides, Dan Ariely, and Nils Olsen, "Contextual and Procedural Determinants of Partner Selection: On Asymmetric Dominance and Prominence," *Social Cognition* (1999).

Chapter 2: The Fallacy of Supply and Demand

BASED ON

Dan Ariely, George Loewenstein, and Drazen Prelec, "Coherent Arbitrariness: Stable Demand Curves without Stable Preferences," *Quarterly Journal of Economics* (2003).

Dan Ariely, George Loewenstein, and Drazen Prelec, "Tom Sawyer and the Construction of Value," *Journal of Economic Behavior and Organization* (2006).

RELATED READINGS

Case Sunstein, Daniel Kahneman, David Schkade, and Ilana Ritov, "Predictably Incoherent Judgments," *Stanford Law Review* (2002).

Uri Simonsohn, "New Yorkers Commute More Everywhere: Contrast Effects in the Field," *Review of Economics and Statistics* (2006).

Uri Simonsohn and George Loewenstein, "Mistake #37: The Impact of Previously Faced Prices on Housing Demand," *Economic Journal* (2006).

Chapter 3: The Cost of Zero Cost

BASED ON

Kristina Shampanier and Dan Ariely, "How Small Is Zero Price? The True Value of Free Products," *Marketing Science* (2007).

RELATED READINGS

Daniel Kahneman and Amos Tversky, "Prospect Theory: An Analysis of Decision under Risk," *Econometrica* (1979).

Eldar Shafir, Itamar Simonson, and Amos Tversky, "Reason-Based Choice," *Cognition* (1993).

Chapter 4: The Cost of Social Norms

BASED ON

Uri Gneezy and Aldo Rustichini, "A Fine Is a Price," *Journal of Legal Studies* (2000).

James Heyman and Dan Ariely, "Effort for Payment: A Tale of Two Markets," *Psychological Science* (2004).

Kathleen Vohs, Nicole Mead, and Miranda Goode, "The Psychological Consequences of Money," *Science* (2006).

RELATED READINGS

Alan Fiske, "The Four Elementary Forms of Sociality: Framework for a Unified Theory of Social Relations," *Psychological Review* (1992).

Pankaj Aggarwal, "The Effects of Brand Relationship Norms on Consumer Attitudes and Behavior," *Journal of Consumer Research* (2004).

Chapter 5: The Influence of Arousal

BASED ON

Dan Ariely and George Loewenstein, "The Heat of the Moment: The Effect of Sexual Arousal on Sexual Decision Making," *Journal of Behavioral Decision Making* (2006).

RELATED READINGS

George Loewenstein, "Out of Control: Visceral Influences on Behavior," *Organizational Behavior and Human Decision Processes* (1996).

Peter H. Ditto, David A. Pizarro, Eden B. Epstein, Jill A. Jacobson, and Tara K. McDonald, "Motivational Myopia: Visceral Influences on Risk Taking Behavior," *Journal of Behavioral Decision Making* (2006).

Chapter 6: The Problem of Procrastination and Self-Control
BASED ON

Dan Ariely and Klaus Wertenbroch, "Procrastination, Deadlines, and Performance: Self-Control by Precommitment," *Psychological Science* (2002).

RELATED READINGS

Ted O'Donoghue and Mathew Rabin, "Doing It Now or Later," *American Economic Review* (1999).

Yaacov Trope and Ayelet Fishbach, "Counteractive Self-Control in Overcoming Temptation," *Journal of Personality and Social Psychology* (2000).

Chapter 7: The High Price of Ownership
BASED ON

Ziv Carmon and Dan Ariely, "Focusing on the Forgone: How Value Can Appear So Different to Buyers and Sellers," *Journal of Consumer Research* (2000).

James Heyman, Yesim Orhun, and Dan Ariely, "Auction Fever: The Effect of Opponents and Quasi-Endowment on Product Valuations," *Journal of Interactive Marketing*

(2004).

RELATED READINGS

Dick Thaler, "Toward a Positive Theory of Consumer Choice," *Journal of Economic Behavior and Organization* (1980).

Daniel Kahneman, Jack Knetsch, and Dick Thaler, "Experimental Tests of the Endowment Effect and the Coase Theorem," *Journal of Political Economy* (1990).

Chapter 8: Keeping Doors Open

BASED ON

Jiwoong Shin and Dan Ariely, "Keeping Doors Open: The Effect of Unavailability on Incentives to Keep Options Viable," *Management Science* (2004).

RELATED READINGS

Sheena Iyengar and Mark Lepper, "When Choice Is Demotivating: Can One Desire Too Much of a Good Thing?" *Journal of Personality and Social Psychology* (2000).

Daniel Gilbert and Jane Ebert, "Decisions and Revisions: The Affective Forecasting of Changeable Outcomes," *Journal of Personality and Social Psychology* (2002).

Ziv Carmon, Klause Wertenbroch, and Marcel Zeelenberg, "When Deliberating Makes Choosing Feel Like Losing," *Journal of Consumer Research* (2003).

Chapter 9: The Effect of Expectations

BASED ON

John Bargh, Mark Chen, and Lara Burrows, "Automaticity of Social Behavior: Direct Effects of Trait Construct and Stereotype Activation on Action," *Journal of Personality and*

Social Psychology (1996).

Margaret Shin, Todd Pittinsky, and Nalini Ambady, "Stereotype Susceptibility: Identity Salience and Shifts in Quantitative Performance," *Psychological Science* (1999).

Sam McClure, Jian Li, Damon Tomlin, Kim Cypert, Latané Montague, and Read Montague, "Neural Correlates of Behavioral Preference for Culturally Familiar Drinks," *Neuron* (2004).

Leonard Lee, Shane Frederick, and Dan Ariely, "Try It, You'll Like It: The Influence of Expectation, Consumption, and Revelation on Preferences for Beer," *Psychological Science* (2006).

Marco Bertini, Elie Ofek, and Dan Ariely, "To Add or Not to Add? The Effects of Add-Ons on Product Evaluation," Working Paper, HBS (2007).

RELATED READINGS

George Loewenstein, "Anticipation and the Valuation of Delayed Consumption," *Economic Journal* (1987).

Greg Berns, Jonathan Chappelow, Milos Cekic, Cary Zink, Giuseppe Pagnoni, and Megan Martin-Skurski, "Neurobiological Substrates of Dread," *Science* (2006).

Chapter 10: The Power of Price

BASED ON

Leonard Cobb, George Thomas, David Dillard, Alvin Merendino, and Robert Bruce, "An Evaluation of Internal Mammary Artery Ligation by a Double-Blind Technic," *New England Journal of Medicine* (1959).

Bruce Moseley, Kimberly O'Malley, Nancy Petersen, Terri Menke, Baruch Brody, David Kuykendall, John Hollingsworth, Carol Ashton, and Nelda Wray, "A Controlled Trial of Arthroscopic Surgery for Osteoarthritis of the Knee," *New England Journal of Medicine* (2002).

Baba Shiv, Ziv Carmon, and Dan Ariely, "Placebo Effects of Marketing Actions: Consumers May Get What They Pay For," *Journal of Marketing Research* (2005).

Rebecca Waber, Baba Shiv, Ziv Carmon, and Dan Ariely, "Paying More for Less Pain," Working paper, MIT (2007).

RELATED READINGS
Tor Wager, James Rilling, Edward Smith, Alex Sokolik, Kenneth Casey, Richard Davidson, Stephen Kosslyn, Robert Rose, and Jonathan Cohen, "Placebo-Induced Changes in fMRI in the Anticipation and Experience of Pain," *Science* (2004).

Alia Crum and Ellen Langer, "Mind-Set Matters: Exercise and the Placebo Effect," *Psychological Science* (2007).

Chapters 11 and 12: The Context of Our Character, Parts I and II

BASED ON
Nina Mazar and Dan Ariely, "Dishonesty in Everyday Life and its Policy Implications," *Journal of Public Policy and Marketing* (2006).

Nina Mazar, On Amir, and Dan Ariely, "The Dishonesty of Honest People: A Theory of Self-Concept Maintenance," *Journal of Marketing Research* (2008).

RELATED READINGS
Max Bazerman and George Loewenstein, "Taking the Bias out of Bean Counting," *Harvard Business Review* (2001).

Maz Bazerman, George Loewenstein, and Don Moore, "Why Good Accountants Do Bad Audits: The Real Problem

Isn't Conscious Corruption. It's Unconscious Bias," *Harvard Business Review* (2002).

Maurice Schweitzer and Chris Hsee, "Stretching the Truth: Elastic Justification and Motivated Communication of Uncertain Information," *Journal of Risk and Uncertainty* (2002).

Chapter 13: Free Lunches
BASED ON
Dan Ariely and Yonatan Levav, "Sequential Choice in Group Settings: Taking the Road Less Traveled and Less Enjoyed," *Journal of Consumer Research* (2000).

Eric. J. Johnson and Daniel Goldstein, "Do Defaults Save Lives?" Science, Vol. 302 (2003), 1338–1339.

Dick Thaler and Shlomo Benartzi, "Save More Tomorrow: Using Behavioral Economics to Increase Employee Savings," *Journal of Political Economy* (2004).

Notes

1. Jodi Kantor, "Entrees Reach $40," *New York Times* (October 21, 2006).
2. Itamar Simonson, "Get Closer to Your Customers by Understanding How They Make Choices," *California Management Review* (1993).
3. Louis Uchitelle, "Lure of Great Wealth Affects Career Choices," *New York Times* (November 27, 2006).
4. Katie Hafner, "In the Web World, Rich Now Envy the Superrich," *New York Times* (November 21, 2006).
6. Valerie Ulene, "Car Keys? Not So Fast," *Los Angeles Times* (January 8, 2007).
7. John Leland, "Debtors Search for Discipline through Blogs," *New York Times* (February 18, 2007).
8. Colin Schieman, "The History of Placebo Surgery," University of Calgary (March 2001).
9. Margaret Talbot, "The Placebo Prescription," *New York Times* (June 9, 2000).

10. Sarah Bakewell, "Cooking with Mummy," *Fortean Times* (July 1999).
11. *Lancet* (April 12, 2003).
12. "Off-Label Use of Prescription Drugs Should Be Regulated by the FDA," Harvard Law School, Legal Electronic Archive (December 11, 2006).
13. Irving Kirsch, "Antidepressants Proven to Work Only Slightly Better Than Placebo," *Prevention and Treatment* (June 1998).
14. Sheryl Stolberg, "Sham Surgery Returns as a Research Tool," *New York Times* (April 25, 1999).
15. Margaret E. O'Kane, National Committee for Quality Assurance, letter to the editor, *USA Today* (December 11, 2006).
16. Federal Bureau of Investigation, *Crime in the United States 2004—Uniform Crime Reports* (Washington, D. C.: U.S. Government Printing Office, 2005).
17. Brody Mullins, "No Free Lunch: New Ethics Rules Vex Capitol Hill," *Wall Street Journal* (January 29, 2007).
18. "Pessimism for the Future," *California Bar Journal* (November 1994).
19. Maryland Judicial Task Force on Professionalism Jan and Crosthwaite, "Moral Expertise: A Problem in the Professional Ethics of Professional Ethicists," *Bioethics*, Vol. 9 (1995): 361–379. (November 10, 2003).
20. Florida Bar/Josephson Institute Study (1993).
21. *DPA Correlator*, Vol. 9, No. 3 (September 9, 2002). See also "The Decline in Professionalism—A Threat to the Future of the American Association of Petroleum Geologists," *Explorer* (May 2004).
22. Jan Crosthwaite, "Moral Expertise: A Problem in the Professional Ethics of Professional Ethicists." *PubMed*

(October 1995).

23. The 2006 Transparency International Corruption Perceptions Index, Highbeam Resea, Pearson Education, and Hrishikesh Vinod, Fordham University Institute for Ethics and Economic Policy.

24. McKinsey and Company, "Payments: Charting a Course to Profits" (December 2005).